D1603873

DOERS:
New Game-Changers

Tom E. Jones

Doers: New Game-Changers

Authored by Tom E. Jones

Illustrated by Cullen D. Jones

ISBN 978-0-9649080-4-8

WORx Publishing
P.O. Box 5637
Carmel CA.
93921

www.worxinc.com

Table of Contents

Reviews

I wish I had had this book in college to prepare me for the challenges that would be faced in the workforce. A helpful guide for dealing with coworkers and bosses of all types, this would could have been a class in and of itself.

Maggie M. Franz

Despite this being a business book, there is lot to be gained from it as one interacts in professional, civic and religious organizations as well. Harnessing the power and abilities of doers could positively impact any organization.

Christina Severinghaus

Tom Jones brings 30+ years of wisdom to his latest project, which is an important treatise on why an organization needs to understand its internal outliers to thrive and compete successfully in an increasing global economy.

Dalitso Ruwe

This is a practical book with lots of wisdom. It explores various types of personalities, gives examples, and is a very apt read for people working in the corporate structure. The author's writing style is simple and to the point.

Naga Narayanaswamy

This book is a handy guide to navigating the turbulent waters of today's workplace. It has practical advice written in a common sense voice. Doers can use this guide to help shape the organizations that accept and encourage them.

Rachel Sandberg

I can attest to Tom's message to the doers, being one myself and knowing the stress that one can have working in an organization not conducive to the doer's attitude of getting things done.

Charles "Vince" Headley

Readers will get invaluable advice on how it can be for leaders and organizations that seek to maximize success in service to their mission and clients.

Dana Wilkie

Conversationally delivered, this book offers methods that both sides of the table can act upon and procedures that will breathe life into suffering workplace relations while simultaneously boosting productivity.

Anthony Rochon

This book is very refreshing. Not only does it touch on both perspectives of the employer and employee, but it also bridges the gap between them.

Early Boykins

This is a very succinct and helpful book. I ended up bookmarking several sections. I particularly enjoyed the sections on Change and on Dysfunction and find them most useful at this time, although the other sections will continue to be useful in the future.

Denise Morse

An immensely practical guide for doers and managers fortunate enough to have doers on their staff. It provides an easy to read, easy to apply road map to help doers work more effectively in today's business climate and to help managers retain doers by keeping them motivated. Tom Jones has once again demonstrated he is a master of organizational leadership.

Steve Keyser

List of Images

Foreword

The title of this revelatory book invites questions. Who are these Doers and exactly where are they? The author directly addresses such questions. We learn that Doers can be found in every organization at every level.

If Doers are the "new game-changers," you may ask, why is my company struggling? This book describes the characteristics and dynamics of Doers plus how to unleash their tremendous potential to get things done when others cannot.

Jones shines the light on personnel who can make a big difference, but who are hiding in plain sight. So, if you look around and identify a Doer nearby, you can facilitate fuller expression of his or her strengths to benefit both employer and employee.

In what ways are Doers like knights? First, knights traditionally are highly motivated to serve, and accomplish their mission. Second, knights bring with them a set of skills and attitudes to their tasks not found elsewhere.

In looking at knights as game-changers in chess, there are many parallels to Doers. To start with, knights can control the middle of the chessboard, and are especially effective when used in combination with other pieces.

Strategic collaboration between knights multiplies their impact. Being uniquely able to leapfrog other pieces on the board gives the knight, if properly positioned, the flexibility and agility to make creative moves.

Since the knight can move in an L-shaped manner rather than straight ahead, its movement is nonlinear. It is this "nonlinearity" that becomes so important in the hands of a skilled player—as in the case of Doers wisely deployed. A Doer placed in a challenging situation can achieve the unexpected if properly supported.

Doers make moves that count. They protect and advance the company's competitive advantage. In a supportive environment where the culture understands and trusts the power of a Doer, he or she becomes a clear-cut asset.

Now having the Doer concept as defined by the author, small businesses as well as large corporations would do well to mount specific efforts to recruit and retain an increasing number/proportion of Doers.

Ken Pascal, Ph.D.

Careermentors, Houston

11

Introduction

The Truth Will Set You Free

A problem cannot be solved with the same consciousness that created it. One must reach to truth outside the system in order to change it. It is the function of consciousness to reach for the truth. – Albert Einstein

According to *The Big Shift*, a worldwide study published by Deloitte University Press, "The success of the modern organization will depend upon its ability to create an environment that cultivates learning and accelerated performance improvement."

In his best seller, *The Purpose Driven Life*, Rick Warren provides a parallel conclusion: "The world needs contribution. We don't just need communication, compassion, and consideration. We need people of action and a bias for achievement."

An American Management Association survey of 800 executives concluded, "The emphasis over the past years has been on high tech skills like math and science, but what's missing is the ability to collaborate and make key decisions at lower levels."

Why CEOs Fail, a FORTUNE magazine cover story (June, 1999), investigated the firing of thirty-eight Fortune 500 top executives. All were smart and had great vision. A two-pronged weakness brought them down: failure to put the right people in the right jobs and not fixing people problems in time to prevent negative outcomes.

Harnessing the Power of Doers

Companies that rely solely on the CEO to navigate the uncharted waters of global competition are floundering.

The validity of this bold assertion is supported by three best-selling business books each based upon the findings of a Stanford University research team headed by professor/author Jim Collins:

Good To Great: Why Some Companies Make the Leap (2001). Compared 1,400 companies once listed on the Fortune 500 to find only eleven that met the criteria necessary to qualify as "great."

How The Mighty Fall: And Why Some Companies Never Give In (2009). Amidst the desolate landscape of fallen great companies, Jim Collins began to wonder: Can decline be detected early and avoided? How can companies reverse course?

Great By Choice: Uncertainty, Chaos, and Luck; Why Some Thrive Despite Them All (2011). A nine-year study analyzed 20,400 companies and identified only seven that have what it takes to succeed in tumultuous times.

These revealing discoveries provide ample evidence it is time to consider a new way of getting results that fully utilizes what Doers bring to the workplace. Positioning them as problem solvers, peer coaches, and change agents will ensure a prosperous future for the organization savvy enough to do so.

Doers are the driving force for innovation; those disruptive game-changers envied and feared by competitors. They supply the initiative for new ideas and the positive energy behind better outcomes. When provided with reasonable opportunities Doers will deliver amazing things.

The survivability of a competitive enterprise hinges upon its ability to harness the power of Doers. Deployed strategically Doers can halt decline and restore prosperity.

Doers hold the key to sustainable success in today's workplace. Regrettably, however, these highly desirable people are in short supply and are also hard to recognize. As you sort through applicants keep an eye out for prospects who are known to:

- Reach across departmental boundaries to build coalitions and create alliances.
- Motivate others by their propensity to enjoy what they do and have fun doing it.
- Operate independently with little direction and limited supervision.
- Accept difficult assignments that others cannot or will not do.
- Seek opportunities to grow personally and develop professionally.

Those charged with executing the corporate vision need to hear the truth from those directly involved in the production of goods and services.

Doers are in the best position to recognize performance, productivity, and process problems and to recommend pragmatic solutions to those with the authority to take corrective action.

Doers are willing to point out what is not working and why, but they must first be assured that they are not putting themselves at risk of retaliation and that they are not wasting their time voicing their concerns.

The following examples demonstrate how the collective voice of the Doers was applied to achieve positive results in four challenging situations:

- A Midwest manufacturer converted $800,000 in monthly product waste into an equivalent amount in new sales by forming Doer-guided Process Improvement Teams in all departments. Their recommended changes in the production and engineering processes resulted in a significant improvement to the bottom line.

- A public sector Family Support Division formed Doers into Performance Management Teams to develop an in-house training program. The results raised their previous ranking of 52nd in productivity to 1st among 53 competing agencies. Their astonishing 491% improvement won national and statewide recognition.

- The largest medical imaging center in the nation successfully downsized three times over three years without damaging its world-class reputation for diagnostic excellence. Management formed a Transition Monitoring Team of Doers from each department to advise the Board of Directors on the reduction in force.

- When the founder of a children's center serving 3,000 families of children with Down's syndrome retired after 30 years, a Doer-lead Strategic Management Team implemented a future-focused planning process that enabled management and staff to hold fast to the founder's vision while the Board selected her replacement.

Hiring Doers Requires Special Effort

Using traditional interview panels whereby those candidates who make the best impression get hired is not likely to bring many Doers to the surface.

LinkedIn founder Reid Hoffman, author of *The Alliance*, believes employers put too much weight on interviews and too little weight on references. "References actually tell you how people work, what their work ethic is. That is a critical piece of data that cannot be put aside or done casually."

In *Work Rules*, a new book disclosing Google's hiring successes, Laszlo Bock promotes a peer-guided selection process that digs deeper into behavioral patterns, work history, personal accomplishments, and growth potential in order to find the most suitable candidates.

Finding good people and keeping them requires that you are known in their network as a place where Doers flourish [They spread the word to other Doers].

The enduring workplace attractions are opportunities to grow in their profession, to make a noticeable difference that matters, and to accomplish something within your company that they could not achieve where they are.

Doers seek assurance that honesty counts and that they can speak truth to authority without fear of retribution. They trust a mistake can be corrected without fear it will be held against them.

Bringing Doers on board may sound positive, but there are costs attached which the organization must take into account. Each of these tendencies has the potential to be problematic:

1. *Doers confront authority, question ambiguity, and expose inconsistency.*
   They challenge directives whenever they believe their way is better. Such behavior may seem irreverent and disrespectful until you consider the benefit of receiving honest feedback from those fully vested in the outcome.

2. *Doers risk losing personal influence and peer support when promoted.*
   Moving them up the career ladder may jeopardize the respect, admiration, and cooperation they receive from coworkers. Creating reward systems for Doers based on their accomplishments rather than on their position can minimize the negative effects of advancement.

3. *Doers may seek opportunities elsewhere when dissatisfied with the lack of enjoyable assignments.*
   This is the most critical factor in keeping doers from jumping ship. Doers network to stay current on job openings. Lacking the potential for personal growth and professional development, Doers are known to seek such opportunities elsewhere.

Be prepared, attracting Doers is not going to be easy. It is a job seeker's market. The best candidates will check out your track record before they agree to interview. The challenge is to establish a reputation as a place where they are eager to come and have reason to stay. Publicly recognizing the value of what Doers have to offer will increase the prospects for bringing in high impact talent.

What This Book Has to Offer

This book presents an exciting new line of thought that focuses on the critical role Doers play from launching an organization to keeping it from running aground. The chapters that follow address the challenges facing Doers and those who employ them.

Readers from the boardroom to the break room are provided with the ways and the means to make the highest and best use of their desire to do the right thing the right way for the right reason.

Managers will come away with a better understanding of why the success of their organization will be determined by the way these high performers are supervised.

If you have employees under your supervision that fit the descriptions above, you are now primed to take advantage of your good fortune. This book will show you how.

Should you feel that your personal achievements are unappreciated, unrecognized, and undervalued, or worse yet, get you into trouble with your peers and those higher up, this book will help you understand why that happens and how to avoid it in the future.

Additionally, it shows small business owners how to make the best use of what Doers bring to their workplace by teaching them how to treat the employer-employee relationship as an economic equation where each side's contribution is given equal weight.

Regardless of who you are, where you work or what your position in the hierarchy might be, if you are truly interested in doing a better job, you too will benefit from what this book has to offer.

Chapter 1 — Relationships

The true measure of a good relationship is not that you know and like each other, but rather that you can accomplish more collaboratively than individually.

People come and go so quickly these days that you do not get to know them well enough to build a relationship before they are history. Plus, you have no idea whether or not those who do stick around understand their jobs the same way you understand yours.

Adding to the difficulty is the rising level of hostility that has replaced civility in many workplaces. The resulting frustration has placed a strain on relationships. Such antagonistic behavior is not only bothersome; it is also highly disruptive to the normal flow of work.

You sometimes feel as if you are the only one who is able to cope with these distractions and still do your job right. Sandwiched in between the challenge of doing your work well and finding others to work well with, is your feeling that nobody higher up seems to notice or care.

It is a challenge to get the job done right despite the difficulty you may face trying to get along with those around you. Any time you stop to think about your feelings towards the people in your work setting, their personalities are bound to get in your way. This is why it is so hard to work with someone you do not know, do not like, or do not trust.

Rather than groaning about how difficult it is to get along, remember that the only thing that really matters to your boss is how well you do your job. The greatest value you can add to your organization is the ability to work well with others.

Focus on the Bottom Line

Business is not just about managing people, it is also about using fewer resources to produce greater results, which means you and your coworkers are expected to increase production, reduce errors, and provide better customer service.

The reason you were hired is to help the enterprise make the highest and best use of limited resources. It is not who you are that counts; it is what you do that truly matters.

The problem is that you are expected not only to excel at your job, but also to work well with others while you are doing it. Success is measured in terms of your ability to get things done through others, which means that you will be expected to achieve results regardless of how well you get along with your peers.

Relationships must be formed quickly and produce measurable outcomes in short order. Seldom is there enough time to truly get to know a colleague before you are both called to action. The work needs to get done regardless of how you feel about each other.

Although it is not easy, you can learn to work collaboratively with almost anyone once you understand the guiding principles that contribute to a good relationship. To start with, you will need to accept that people bring differing points of view to the same task.

Seeing things differently is just one of many barriers that drive people apart when they should be pulling together. Breaking down these barriers and forming collaborative relationships requires that you consider new ways of thinking about the people who do not agree with you.

At the end of this section, you will read about a set of simple practices that will help you to build a healthy working relationship with just about anyone—even those you think are idiots. But before we get to that, let us first look at some typical personalities that will drive you nuts unless you learn how to work with them.

Working with Quirky Personalities

Whiners

Somebody always seems to be whining about something. Before you tune out a whiner, however, be aware that whining is a sign that someone is having a problem and is asking for help. Given the fast-paced, demanding nature of the modern workplace, where everyone is expected to adjust rapidly and respond accurately under pressure, it is a wonder more people are not whining.

Whiners are sometimes just looking for attention. For many, it is the safest way they know to convey their unhappiness without pointing the finger at someone directly.

What you would really like to do is tell these whiners to grow up and get back to work. That would not likely do any good even if it were an accepted behavior. What you need to do instead is get these folks to join you in solving the organization's problems rather than their own.

Slackers

As a rule of thumb, the more important meeting goals and producing quality work becomes, the more Doers are likely to complain about their backsliding coworkers.

As tempting as it is to plug the leaks in the payroll or get rid of the dead wood; firing people for nonperformance usually is not effective. That is because when slackers get wind that their performance is being monitored, they will pick up the pace just long enough to survive close scrutiny. Once the threat has passed, they return to business as usual.

Slackers have mastered the art of just getting by so do not expect them to give much constructive thought to improving their relationships with you or with their coworkers.

Misfits

Does the same problem keep coming back to you despite your coworker's promise to take care of it? Welcome to the world of misfits where people turn in work that is partially completed or poorly done, hoping someone else will take care of the problem.

Other misfit-type behaviors include coworkers with harmful habits, poor organization skills, or no self-confidence. Misfits also have a history of making bad personal choices. Although such behavior is not new to the workplace, it is becoming more commonplace and increasingly difficult to manage.

Misfits lack the trust to deal openly with coworkers, so they resist structured activities, tend to avoid responsibility, and prefer to be left alone to work at their own pace.

Loners

Like most Doers, you probably take it for granted that your coworkers will form teams and work together cooperatively. The truth is that a significant number of today's workers do not know how to collaborate—it is something they have never been taught.

Some people respond to being taught collectively and tested individually by becoming self-reliant. Seeking opportunities for individual achievement, they sign on for a job valuing only what they can do for themselves—cooperating with you holds no importance.

Loners believe that asking someone for help is cheating. As far back as they can remember anyone caught collaborating was punished both at school and at home.

Building Task-Based Relationships

Forming productive relationships by removing the impediments that separate you from the quirky personalities of your teammates is not likely to happen naturally. The tenets of teamwork described below provide guidelines for building task-based relationships, so that when you encounter whiners, slackers, misfits, or loners the focus is on their task and not on their personalities.

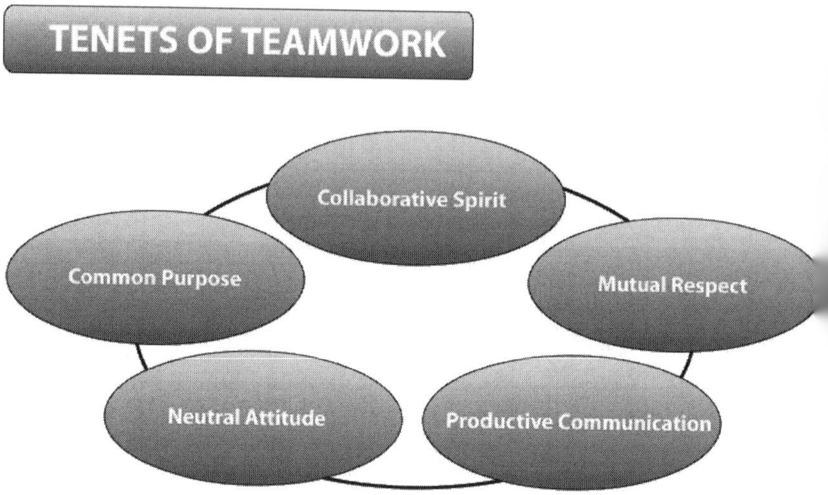

TENETS OF TEAMWORK

Collaborative Spirit

Common Purpose

Mutual Respect

Neutral Attitude

Productive Communication

Figure 1 — Tenets of Teamwork

Collaborative Spirit

You can accomplish more by working together than you can by working alone.

Before you decide to join forces with another person, you have to ask yourself the question: How do I benefit from this relationship? At first glance, there may appear to be very little benefit other than making the other party happy. You may have to dig a little deeper before you discover that you really need what the other person brings to the table. It helps sometimes to list the skill sets you have and compare them to what you know about the other person.

Even if you believe the other person to be incompetent, you will never know for certain until you work along side him or her long enough to confirm your suspicions. Think of it this way: a coworker brings to the job a unique set of abilities, which when matched with yours has the potential for improving the odds that you will both succeed.

Something heartwarming and emotionally uplifting happens when two individuals complete a difficult task that neither could have accomplished without the other. A collaborative spirit emerges that was not there before. Your desire to continue the relationship increases and you all feel motivated to aim higher on the next project.

Common Purpose

Work on the same things at the same time.

Problem solving and decision-making are two separate functions. Working simultaneously on both will create confusion and divert team energy. Solving a problem calls for people who are comfortable recalling intricate details, and remembering forgotten bits and pieces that may help to solve the mystery. It makes sense to begin the search for a solution by sharing your collective memories of what could have caused the deviation from expectations.

Making decisions is more about setting a new course to change in the future. This requires people who are good at thinking forward. In order to develop a common purpose from which to make their decision, teammates must agree to refocus their attention to what lies ahead.

The priority in working with others is to establish a common purpose and focus before you pool your knowledge and begin your work. Without first determining a common purpose, much time and energy will be wasted arguing over who is right and who is wrong. It also increases the chances of missing the point or doing something stupid.

Mutual Respect

Accept and value what others bring to the relationship.

First impressions are not always the ones you want to rely upon when it comes to working with others. You really do not get a clear sense of what another person has to offer until you have given her or him a second and third look.

What others bring to the relationship is a valid expectation of how the task should be accomplished. Something you could not possibly understand unless you invite them to share what they know without fear of being judged prematurely.

The objective is to focus on the sources of the differing viewpoints and not to persuade others to change their way of thinking. After all, you cannot change what others think unless you first understand the basis for their thoughts. It is important to understand how the views of others were formed.

A mutual exploration of individual expectations is an opportunity to clarify everyone's position while gaining a better understanding of what each person anticipates will happen when the actual work begins.

Productive Communication

Clarify what you mean and what actions you expect others to take.

Everything you say or do not say has meaning. The challenge is to communicate in a manner that clearly conveys your intentions and leaves no doubt as to what you expect from others.

Task-oriented relationships thrive on accurate information, so it is important that you say what you mean, mean what you say, and not make any commitments you unable or unprepared to keep.

Accurate information travels best with those you know to be reliable transmitters and receivers. It is critical to identify others who are trustworthy and communicate with them directly rather than through intermediaries.

Tell them you want to know the truth about what they are hearing from other sources. Let them know that if you find out they modified or withheld the facts, you will not rely on them again.

Neutral Attitude

When faced with disagreement, avoid taking a position until you know the whole story.

Conflict is a sign that something critical to the relationship is missing. Rather than argue over what you think you know, wait until you have updated each other on what has transpired since you last joined forces. People and circumstances change, so there is a good possibility that you may be lacking current information.

When a conflict occurs, listen first in order to establish a clear understanding of what is keeping you apart. Start looking for sources of new information to help you form new opinions. If you cannot resolve the issue quickly, set it aside and do not let it interfere with completing the task.

Disagreements provide a natural opportunity for teammates to identify their differences. The key objective is to agree to disagree until subsequent clarification is forthcoming.

Benefits

Doers often disparage workplace relationships because they do not know, do not like, or do not trust the people with whom they work. Applying the tenets of teamwork when building a task-based relationship objectifies rather than personalizes individual performance. This shift in focus attracts Doers because it is now clear to them what, not who, needs to be fixed.

What follows, then, is the assurance that your efforts are recognized, your contributions are valued, your job is more fun, and your organization really is a great place to work. Strained relationships, which were once a source of pain, now become a source of pride and joy.

Promoting Doer Dialogue

Once the tenets of teamwork are put into practice and the team formation process begins to take shape, the next step is to develop an on-going dialogue between and among the Doers within each team. The purpose of the React—Respond—Reflect process model outlined below is to encourage more listening and less speaking during Doer team interactions. Those who practice this process find that they become an even more effective performer by being quick to listen and slow to speak.

React! Suppress first impressions or impulses. Expressing your feelings and thoughts prematurely shifts the focus away from the speaker and discourages rather than encourages a more thorough exploration of the issue. The temptation to react when a thought crosses your mind is natural, but it should be held in check to encourage the speaker to continue.

Respond!   Answer positively or affirmatively. The appropriate time to respond will become obvious once the speaker has expressed what is foremost on his or her mind. A positive response not only acknowledges that you have heard what has been said thus far, but also encourages the speaker to respond more openly to your questions and concerns.

Reflect!   Suggest alternatives or resolutions. The opportunity to reflect on alternative outcomes and explore potential solutions will surface naturally when critical judgment is suspended and the dialogue is free flowing between all participants. At this point, you can hold up the mirror so that everyone benefits from seeing the situation through multiple sets of eyes.

Achievers draw their sense of purpose and pride of accomplishment from their team-based relationships in a high performance workplace. In a dysfunctional organization, however, where their achievements matter little, relying on the same support system to meet their personal needs can be risky.

Attending To Your Needs

During a period of organizational unraveling, with people moving up, moving down, and moving out, it is critical to your health and welfare to have a personal support system in place to help you cope with the challenges of change.

Counting on those around you for support is not always useful if they are also caught up in problems of their own. As your organization and the people it employs grapple with marketplace demands, you must look to other sources to reaffirm your own relevance and purpose.

In his book, *Healing the Wounds: Overcoming the Trauma of Layoffs and Revitalizing Downsized Organizations,* David Noer refers to the concept of having all of one's needs met by the organization as the "taproot strategy." Noer poses several thought provoking questions, including, "What happens if the taproot gets cut? If who you are is where you work, what are you if you lose your job?"

Organizationally dependent people, he says, "rely on an employer to nurture all aspects of their life. Their self-esteem, identity, and social worth are nourished by a single organization." When released from their jobs or moved to unfamiliar assignments, these people see no meaning to their lives.

Another thing to bear in mind: as you change, your support system must change with you. People in your current support system, if you have one, support you because they like who and what you are right now— they may not want you to change. In fact, they will frequently work against you if you try to change.

So, how do you get the support you need if you can no longer count on people in the workplace? You build your own support system—one that meets your needs.

Support System: Functions And Players

Assembling your support system takes time and requires a great deal of thought. Think of it as a series of "casting calls." People audition and you carefully consider who would be the best person to play each part. The process works best if you let people know what role you would like them to assume, and, should they agree, what you expect them to do when you call on them for support.

Unlike mentoring or networking, your support system will focus on you as a person, rather than on your job or career. The primary mode of communication between yourself and the "players" in your support system should be one-on-one. At times, the level of interaction can be intense, particularly during periods of doubt and confusion.

Often, when you are not sure of what is really "bugging" you, exploring the deeper aspects of problems with someone in your support system will bring the real issue to the surface so you can face it honestly. This is particularly helpful when you are struggling to overcome your own misgivings and misconceptions.

The following descriptions of support system roles were developed from the research and writings of pioneers in the career development field. The six roles presented here have been specifically selected to fit the needs of Doers who might be suffering and are in need of confirmation and clarity.

Confidence Builder: The key function of a confidence builder is to provide encouragement when you need a lift. Choose people who respect you for who you are, not for what you do. People who know you well are better able to sense when your spirits need a boost. Most Doers rely on their own self-confidence to get them through the rough spots. However, when the rough spots turn into tough times, it is comforting to know people who can supply you with the assurance you need to get back on track.

Challenger: This role requires someone who will question your flight plan if they think you need a course correction. You frequently need a sturdy sounding board to test your notions, thoughts, and ideas. The stronger your convictions are, the more people you will need to fill this role. Finding people who will say no, if no really is the best answer, is not an easy assignment. Just as you demand much of yourself, so must you demand much from the challengers in your support system. You will place demands on their time to listen to you, on their intellect to take you seriously, and on their willpower to refute your assumptions.

Motivator: Doers need relationships with people who stimulate their thinking and prompt them when they need a reality check. Motivators are like a starter on an engine—particularly useful when, after a period of idleness, you need a quick burst of energy to get moving again. Pick people who inspire you and build you up. They do not have to know you to be helpful. Authors, artists, poets, preachers, prophets, gurus, or just about anyone who provides a positive influence qualifies as a motivator.

Sustainer: The sustainer is concerned for your welfare and your wellbeing. Just like the body, the mind needs nourishment to grow and develop. When your mental health sags, you need someone who will not just prop you up, but lift you up. You need to know that there are people who care what happens to you. Helping you look for opportunity in adversity is one way that sustainers can help you to broaden and develop your horizons.

Friend: Friends are people who care for you and admire the way you are. They see you as a special person and do not try to change you. You can trust them to respect your point of view, even if they disagree with it. They openly discuss their personal concerns and easily express their frank opinions. Spending time with your friends provides a source of satisfaction and stimulation rarely found in any other relationship.

Reflector: These are people who think like you, have the same interests as you, and agree with you on important issues. Because they are like you in many ways and value many of the same things you do, they serve as a "mirror" reflecting your thoughts and feelings. You are comfortable bouncing ideas around in their presence without fear of judgment or criticism. They accept your faults and forgive your mistakes because they respect you.

Career development authority, Beverly Kaye, recommends limiting the number of support roles you assign to any one person. The convenience of going to a single source for a variety of support needs is overshadowed by the possibility of stressing out that special person by expecting him or her to wear too many hats.

Finding people willing to provide the support you need right now should be a priority. Take the time to fill in a partial list of potential candidates for each category and keep it updated as your need for support changes. The time you invest in building a support system can provide you with a great source of independent strength and courage as you strive to overcome the challenges facing you in the ever-changing workplace.

Chapter 2 — Competence

The situation that Doers dread most is being teamed with someone who lacks the skill, ability, and motivation to do the right things, the right way, for the right reason.

Such people are labeled as incompetents who walk around in a fog unaware of the negative impact they are having on those around them. They may not be willfully stupid nor do they screw up intentionally, but they continue to make costly mistakes every day.

As tempting as it is to write off these non-performers as incompetents, consider instead that they are just people who at various times simply do not know what they are expected to do; or if they do know, they do not know how to do it right; or if they do know how to do it right, they see no particular benefit in doing it that way.

When you find yourself in a situation where working with such a person is forced upon you, this chapter will show you how to make the most of your predicament.

What you do with the information that follows will depend upon how attached you are to your job, your compensation, and your company. If you have other reasons to be dissatisfied, then, why put up with incompetent coworkers as well?

After thoughtful reflection, you may decide that the situation is hopeless and there is nothing anyone can do. Now is a good time to consider changing jobs or transferring to another department.

On the other hand, if you like your job and are happy with your workplace, then you have three viable options:

1) Grin and bear it, look the other way, and just put up with the situation in the hope that the incompetent may be found out and fired.

2) Make a serious effort to try to change his or her behavior. Go over his or her head perhaps or lodge a complaint with the human resource department.

3) Change the way you deal with incompetency, which affords you the luxury of experimenting with a variety of methods and doing so at your own pace.

If you selected options #1 or #2, then you may not find the chapter very practical. Although, it will provide you with a wider perspective of the issues you face, you are not likely to change someone else's behavior.

If you chose option #3, you are about to learn specific strategies and practical techniques for dealing with any and all incompetent coworkers, and how best to approach and/or work with them in order to achieve your goals and theirs too. You will also learn how to use The Competency Index to help you achieve your objective.

Competency Index

The Competency Index (CI) is a simple measure that gauges how deeply ingrained someone's behavior might be. It enables you to determine which skills he or she is missing and which you will need to bring to the relationship in order to make it work.

What follows are recommended strategies to use for each of these levels. Keep in mind that these are not bad people; they just behave in an incompetent manner under certain conditions or when placed in particular situations.

Incompetent people tend to be set in their ways and may not appreciate the need for doing anything differently. It will be difficult to influence a change in their behavior, but there are practical steps to be taken that might make a difference.

Level 5   Finally gets it but it took some time

Level 4   Occasionally gets it but needs reminding

Level 3   Gets it after being hit over the head with it

Level 2   Might get it if there is a personal benefit

Level 1   Does not get it, and probably never will

Figure 2 — Competency Index

To make the situation a bit more realistic, imagine yourself as the Doer in each of the following true-life stories.

Level 1: Does Not Get It and Probably Never Will

Situation

You are working as a product manager for a major paper products company. Ed, your counterpart in marketing, is not providing the information your staff needs to do their job effectively.

The problem with Ed is that you hardly ever see him. His manner is usually cold and unapproachable and his office door is always closed. His comments at the task team meetings tend to be judgmental and fault finding. You get the feeling that he is totally insensitive to your needs.

You feel frustrated because Ed has made sure that he is the only conduit for information flowing upward to top management. He also never invites participation in any major decisions; in most cases, he has already determined the course of action to be taken and simply announces his decision at the weekly meeting.

You can appreciate that Ed's cultivation of top management may be a good thing for his department. However, you feel that his lack of collaboration is making your staff feel resentful, frustrated, and demoralized.

Strategy

In Ed's case, you are certain that he is a Level 1 candidate because he is not interested in hearing anyone else's view and he is not likely to have many insights of his own either. He truly believes he is right and he sees no reason to seek information from outside sources. So, before Ed's mind can be changed, it must first be opened.

Still, before you decide the situation is hopeless, here are some steps that may help you get what you need from Ed:

1) Arrange a mutually convenient discussion over lunch or after hours. Meeting in his office gives him control, so your best bet is to select a neutral site off campus.

2) Ask him for his help in resolving a problem, in this case, departmental morale. For example, what can he do to involve himself more with your staff?

3) Present the situation as factually and unemotionally as possible. Do not speculate on how others may feel or on what he needs to do.

4) Avoid any direct criticism, since that will be counterproductive.

5) If he challenges your assessment of the situation, do not waste your time arguing.

Let some time elapse and see if there is any change in behavior. If he does change for the better, arrange another meeting when you can provide new information, positive feedback, and encouragement. Be prepared to restate your position as if it were the first time.

If there is no change, you know that things are likely to continue as before. Taking the issue to a higher level, even with documented support, is really not an option. Ed is well connected at the top, so any complaints about him are likely to be ignored or backfire on you. So you either accept Ed or dust off your resume in preparation for a job search.

Level 2: Might Get It If There Is A Personal Benefit

Situation

Travis is a braggart and a blowhard. All he ever talks about are his accomplishments, which in fact are not his at all. He seldom has an idea of his own, so he keeps stealing from others — you in particular. You are frustrated because he rarely has anything substantive to say, but the higher-ups are swayed by his charismatic personality and his ability to persuade the big-name clients.

Your problem started when Travis put his hat in the ring for the division head position. The final three candidates were to be interviewed by the Board of Directors — as a member of the screening panel, you know first-hand that his performance was a masterpiece.

He entered the boardroom dressed fashionably perfect, straight from the cover of Fortune magazine. He paused at the door just long enough for all eyes to turn his way. Oozing with charm, he worked the room masterfully, glad-handing the directors and calling them each by name. Travis had done his homework or rather memorized the materials someone had put together for him. He got the job. Good you thought, now he is out of your hair. Not a chance. Shortly after he settled in, he persuaded corporate to place you on a special task force that he was asked to chair.

Strategy

Travis fits into the Level 2 category because he ignored all the signs of impending trouble in his division. Now that your success is tied to his, you might think about the benefits of convincing him that he needs to change his behavior if he expects to rise any higher in the company. That should get his attention.

Before you make your case with Travis, however, you will need to prepare several alternative strategies:

1) Giving him a take-it-or-leave-it choice is not a good idea. Providing him with a list of options offers a better way for him to accept what you say without admitting that he is wrong.

2) Rather than challenge him alone, bring others with you who support your position. It helps if he holds those you select in high regard or has worked with them successfully in the past.

3) An alternative to the collective approach is to have each of your supporters approach him independently with the same or similar message.

4) Put any verbal agreements or commitments he makes in writing using his words. Otherwise, he may deny ever having agreed with what you proposed.

5) Provide testimonials from people he sees as important or prominent either in his profession or in his chain of command. Relevant quotations from public figures and notable personalities whom he admires will also help your case.

Once you have followed these steps, you have achieved your first objective, which is to neutralize any negative feelings he may have toward you or any desire he may have to shoot the messenger. Remember, at this level the incompetent in question may know how to do it right, but does not know why he should because he sees no personal benefit. That being the case your primary objective is to open a closed mind, not to change it. Therefore, be patient, gentle, kind, reverent, forbearing, but do not give up.

Level 3: Gets It After Being Hit Over The Head

Situation

You are the manager of a women's leisurewear boutique, which is part of a national chain. Your store has recently been losing money. In talking with some of the managers, you have come to realize that there are pervasive problems affecting all stores in the chain. When you tried to talk with Carla, the CEO, about what was going on, she told you that you did not see the big picture and not to worry. Her response only makes you worry more.

You feel that the problem originates with Carla, who seems to have no clear idea of what running the company requires. She is always totally immersed in doing what she understands so well—talking with investors and bankers—but she pretty much ignores the management of the business. When new stores fail to meet their sales targets, Carla ignores the problem. Her board of directors, all family members and friends, never question her actions or ask for financial reports. There is no one to coordinate the purchasing activities; inventory management, credit and returns policies, and individual store managers are left to their own devices.

Strategy

In Carla's case, you are dealing with a Level 3, which means she might get it after being hit over the head with it. Because she is smart and ambitious, there is a way to reach her. However, as with the proverbial mule, you first have to get her attention.

Here are some steps that you can take, either alone or jointly with others who share your frustrations:

1) Ask to meet with her in person. Tell her it is important enough that you are willing to travel to her office.

2) Present her with a list of your concerns. Tell her that your colleagues and coworkers have voiced similar concerns.

3) Make her aware of the serious risk of letting things continue. Emphasize that managers will be resigning and the firm may go out of business. If you are prepared to do so, offer to resign if there is no change.

4) Offer your solution, which is to hire an experienced executive to serve as chief operating officer for the parent company.

5) Suggest that by delegating the responsibility for setting, coordinating, and monitoring corporate-wide policies, she would be free to do what she does best which is to attract new investors and raise additional capital.

Your best efforts will not be good enough the first time out. Be prepared to give multiple presentations before seeing progress. You will know you are getting through at this level when the rebuttal shifts from, "Why should I?" to "How can I?" After that it is a matter of providing ample documentation to show how it should be done. Come prepared with examples of how this worked in other places and why you are convinced it is the right thing to do here. Even though it appears to be obvious, you may have to restate your conviction until she finally gets it. You are done. The idea has a new owner, so let it go.

Level 4: Occasionally Gets It But Needs Reminding

Situation

Since reporting to Polly, you have discovered that the old adage is true: it is not what you know, but who you know that counts. Her uncle's position on the Board of Directors made it possible for Polly, a recent graduate with no job experience, to get hired on as a copywriter. As a long-time employee, you were bemused at how quickly Polly advanced from simple copywriting to media buying. When the media director was hired away by a competitor, the CEO of the company appointed Polly to that management position without interviewing any other candidates.

Polly was now in a situation where several of the people reporting to her, including you, have significantly more experience than she does. Aware of the resentment and snickering behind her back, Polly has become autocratic in her management style, which only further widened the gulf between her and your coworkers who report to her.

Strategy

Polly is a good example of a Level 4 incompetent because she is approachable and seems to understand that her ties to her uncle are creating resentment among her colleagues. She tried several times to make it on her own merits but falls back on using her connection with her uncle whenever she encounters any obstacle.

1) Provide a neutral setting for your first attempt to discuss the problem. It is best to meet in in a place familiar to her where she feels comfortable. Lunch at her favorite restaurant is ideal.

2) Allow time for personal chitchat about her life, family, friends, and personal interests. Keep the conversation lite by sharing a personal experience that relates to what you wish to discuss.

3) Seek her feelings on the topic before sharing yours. Let how she feels be your guide for making your point. Accept her assessment, even if it is contrary to your view, before laying out your concerns.

4) Establish your understanding and awareness of how others feel about the situation. Then share your personal feelings and intentions. Lastly, tell her what you would like her to change in the future.

5) Make suggestions for how this situation could be handled differently if she is agreeable to altering her behaviors. Offer to write down the gist of the discussion and send it back to her for confirmation.

Do not get clever with your approach to people like Polly—keep it simple. Avoid high tech presentations. Incompetents at this level are easily befuddled when mentally overloaded. You are far better off repeating the same simple pitch. Give them credit for whatever portion of your pitch they do get, but do not go overboard with praise—it is important to be authentic. Provide regular follow-ups even when there are no issues, otherwise they will forget what they have accepted or agreed to since your last discussion.

Level 5: Finally Gets It But It Took Some Time

Situation

Your boss Willard is a financial genius. His peers call him "Will the Wizard," and they mean it most respectfully. Will has an MBA from the Wharton School and a wall full of certificates and awards attesting to his experience and skills in managing the financial intricacies of a fast-growth company in the information business. A year ago, its stockholders approved a merger with a competitor. Will, who had been the key person in structuring the terms of the merger, was picked by the Board of Directors to be president of the newly formed company.

To you, and obviously to the Board, he seemed like the best choice. The trouble is, as you are now discovering, Will stays in his office with the door closed most of the time.

When you try to make an appointment, you are told that Will is not available—he is away at a conference, or in a meeting offsite, and will get back to you shortly. Shortly never comes. You have evidence that Will is bypassing you by asking for very specific information directly from the people who report to you and then taking actions that undercut your authority.

You are hoping that given time, he will come around. But other direct reports, especially those who had recently transferred from the former competitor, have no such patience. Some plan to approach the CEO of the parent company with their complaints; others just plan to seek employment elsewhere. The fall-out from this discontent surely means that the company is in for a rough ride.

Strategy

It will take time and persistence to eventually make Level 5 incompetents like Will understand the consequences of their behavior. With your insistence, he should be able to adjust his style to bring it more aligned with what you and your peers expect from him and to act in a more responsive manner.

Incompetents at this level pretty much teach themselves and seldom make the same mistake twice. All you have to do is point out the consequences of their behavior and wait patiently.

1) Provide a balanced argument both for and against whatever actions you feel he should take. Include a list of possible consequences to him and the company if nothing changes.

2) Allow him ample opportunity to develop his own solutions and time to experiment with new behaviors. Offer to serve as a participant observer or silent monitor to provide frequent feedback.

3) Assume he will want to verify your perceptions of his behavior, so be accurate and realistic. Do not overstate the issues or report anything that you have not witnessed firsthand.

4) If he disagrees with what you report, make an organized presentation of your position and ask for his perspective on each point.

5) If he accepts your recommendations, submit a step-by-step timetable for whatever changes he has agreed to make and assure him that you will get back to him with the results so there will not be any surprises.

At this level, you are dealing with a person who at various times does not understand what you expect of him or he does not know how to do it right. Persistence rather than persuasion will result in a much higher pay-off. If you do not receive the answer you want, let him know you are not going away until you do.

Different Folks Need Different Strokes

As you learn to apply the Competency Index keep in mind that people who demonstrate incompetence are often lacking knowledge or skills or experience. The Competency Checklist should make it easier for you to identify which competencies a particular person is missing and be in a position to assist him, her, or yourself to develop those skills and abilities most needed for the job.

As you review the checklist, put your introspective "hat" on and think about the competencies you feel are your strengths and those that you may need to develop further.

Competency Checklist

Rate your degree of confidence in either your ability to perform each of the competencies listed below or that of the person you have been asked to rate. Use a five-point scale with (5) being high and (1) being low.

Judgment

___Reaching logical conclusions

___Making quality choices based on limited information

___Identifying pressing needs and setting priorities

___Critically evaluating written communications

Organization

___Planning, scheduling, controlling the work of others

___Using resources economically

___Dealing with paperwork

___Coping with multiple time demands

Analytical

___Searching for relevant data

___Analyzing complex information

___Selecting the most significant elements

___Prioritizing options

Sensitivity

___Perceiving the needs, concerns, problems of others

___Working through conflicts by listening to both sides

___Being tactful when dealing with different personalities

___Dealing effectively with emotional issues

Delegation

___Assessing the reliability and accuracy of subordinates

___Reaching conclusions on implementation strategies

___Assigning actions to the most appropriate person(s)

___Defining standards for performance measurement

Interpersonal

___Listening to and supporting the ideas of others

___Giving and receiving constructive feedback

___Sharing personal feelings and beliefs

___Working productively in teams

Political

___Identifying issues involving formal and informal leaders

___Using corporate policies to achieve goals

___Establishing cooperative relationships with key people

___Realigning power to form new coalitions

Now that you are familiar with the contents of the Competency Checklist above, think about going back over the list; only this time think about those aspects that you are comfortable with and those that you need to develop further.

Each competency is measurable and therefore can be improved. Consider applying your strengths more frequently. Focus on what you do well and look at your less often used skills as potential growth opportunities.

This extra effort will go a long way toward ensuring that your supervisor is not working his or her way through the Competency Index with you in mind.

Footnote: The list of selected skill dimensions contained in the Competency Checklist above was taken in part from The University of California, Berkeley, Assessment Center assessors guide and used here with permission from the Director of Human Resources.

Chapter 3 — Communication

Whenever contact is made, communication occurs. Every time you open your mouth, roll your eyes, purse your lips, nod your head, cross your arms, or clear your throat, someone is going to assign meaning to it. Hand gestures, voice tone, and body posture can send a signal that you like or dislike someone or are happy or unhappy about something. Even silence conveys a message.

Here is a good example. The human resource director of a rapidly growing company in a remote part of the mid-west received a call from an executive recruiter that a recent MBA graduate from a top-tier university would be in town for a short time and would like to arrange an interview.

Not wanting to pass up the opportunity, the director hastily assembled several key people to convene early the next morning. Everyone on this makeshift selection committee was looking forward to meeting such a highly qualified candidate.

Although the candidate's answers to their questions demonstrated a high level of intelligence and solid understanding of what the job entailed, his responses were brief and unenthusiastic. Throughout the interview he was lackadaisical and sometimes sat expressionless as if he was bored.

Not wanting to waste any more time or effort, the director thanked the candidate for coming and closed the interview. After a brief discussion, the committee concluded that the candidate was obviously not interested and voted not to consider him for the position.

Some time later, the human resource director learned that a rival company had hired the candidate who was exceeding all their expectations. A follow-up call to the recruiter further revealed that this stellar candidate did poorly in the interview because his father had died suddenly and he had flown in to arrange the funeral and to look for a job in order to be near his ailing mother.

So, who is to blame here: the candidate for not explaining his circumstances or the interview team for making a judgment based solely on his behavior during the interview?

No doubt, you could share similar misunderstandings from your own work history. If you were to dig a little deeper into these common miscommunications you would likely find that the parties involved probably did not know or trust each other, so neither side put much effort into providing clarification to the other.

Likability and trustworthiness are major factors in determining just how much effort those on either end of the communication link are willing to invest in trying to understand each other.

If you like and trust someone, you tend to overlook that person's faults and shortcomings. You will probably give that person a little slack also when it comes to tolerating his or her quirky traits and annoying habits.

That same courtesy may not be extended to people you neither like nor trust. You are prone to be intolerant and unforgiving of their faults as well. In fact, you tend to view anything these people do or say with a critical eye and a suspicious mind.

Communicating nonjudgmental feedback to someone you neither like nor trust is difficult to achieve without leaving behind hurt feelings. Underachievers and non-performers are not likely to reach Doer status unless you are open, honest, and direct with them.

Providing negative feedback is one-half of the relationship equation; receiving it is the other half. Communicating with potential Doers requires that you do both in order for them to accept what you say as truth and to feel confident acting upon it.

Making Your Point Without Making An Enemy

Doers prefer to tell the truth and expect others to be honest with them in return. More importantly, Doers expect coworkers to communicate bad news graciously and to offer criticism objectively. Timeliness is also a key factor. Waiting for the right moment, or putting it off until the recipient is in a good mood, just compounds the issue. Best to transfer the information while it is fresh and there is still time to rectify the situation.

Fact-based criticism contains important information that can be both useful and growth producing if the recipient does not personalize it. Yes, it sometimes hurts and you may feel some guilt or pain, but it is not about you.

The less reactive you are to criticism, the more honest and direct people will be with you. Both factors are important elements in trust building. The challenge, then, is to encourage coworkers to offer up criticism without putting them through an uncomfortable or embarrassing process.

Criticism is simply the act of reviewing someone else's work and providing him or her with your findings. No one likes how it feels to be criticized, but that does not mean it is without value.

The purpose in giving criticism is to achieve clarity and build trust, not to hurt someone's feelings, but that may happen anyway. The trick is to keep trying until the recipient understands that the message is meant to be helpful, not harmful.

Crafting your message so that it carries no personal blame takes practice. Until you get used to this more direct way of communicating, it might help if you script your message by writing it down and repeating it several times out loud to yourself before you share it.

Such a formal response may seem awkward, especially if you are not used to writing down what you plan to say before you say it. The fact that it is not like you demonstrates your willingness to try something new. It also confirms that you want to change the way things are—a crucial first step in getting your coworkers to take what you say seriously and to act upon it immediately.

Communicating Negative Information

Providing criticism to people of equal rank or status is difficult but doable. They do not have to listen to you and even if they do, they do not have to act upon what you say. Your chances of getting them to accept your point of view will be greatly increased if you select the most appropriate path from one of the following options:

Sympathy

Being sympathetic conveys that you understand how the other person feels, but you do not feel that way yourself. Use this path in situations where you truly want to understand someone's intentions and are trying to accept how that person feels even though you may disagree once you know. This path is not as useful with disgruntled peers because they are less likely to understand their own feelings. All is not lost though; it could be a good beginning. Having their feelings acknowledged without being the focus of blame could open up this path in the future.

Empathy

Being empathetic communicates that you understand how the other person feels because you feel or have felt that way yourself. This path gives you the ability to connect on an emotional level. It shows that you have insights to share and are seeking a deeper exploration of the issues. This path also serves to open up communications with a potential Doer who will be pleased to know you accept his or her point of view but may not be ready to accept yours.

Apathy

Being apathetic indicates that you do not know how the other person feels and do not want to know either. This path works best with people who care more about their own feelings than they do about yours. That being the case, you might as well make your point without regard to their feelings or potential reactions. This path demonstrates that all you want from the other person is acceptance of your position and an understanding that you will be back if you do not get what you need.

When communicating your thoughts is not the issue, but understanding the basis for criticism from others is, you may have to make some adjustments. For instance, in seeking clarification, try not to imply that the criticism is without merit until you hear the details. In addition, when responding to accusations or complaints, take care not to accept responsibility too soon. Until you have developed a list of your own phrases, try these:

SEEKING CLARIFICATION

★ I am confused about what you need from me and when you expect it

★ I am excited about this task, but I need more time to do it right.

★ I am disappointed with these results because I had higher expectations.

★ I am not prepared right now and need time to think about my response.

★ I am reluctant to implement your suggestions without consulting my team.

Figure 3 — Seeking Clarification

Separating Fact From Fiction

What you do not know can, and ultimately does, hurt you and potentially others, too. Instead of keeping negative information hidden, what you want others to do is tell it like it is or at least let you know when something is amiss.

Communicating honestly, even when it raises tempers, will ultimately pull people together and build trust.

Here is a good example of why being straight with people is important. The president of a university gave one of his deans a smaller percentage raise than her colleagues in an attempt to communicate his dissatisfaction with her performance. The University Board of Directors had authorized merit raises of up to 5 percent.

The president reasoned that when the underachieving dean compared her meager 1 percent increase to the maximum 5 percent received by each of her colleagues she would get the message and improve her performance.

She got a message, but not the one he intended. Concerned that she had fallen short of her goals, she was expecting the president to request her resignation.

Imagine her surprise when she received the president's letter announcing a bonus. At first, she felt like a fool for having doubted herself.

Later, she realized that he must have known she had not achieved her goals, but he did not mention that fact in the letter. Either he did not care or she was working for an incompetent boss.

Neither was true of course. The president was fully aware of her shortcomings, but had not communicated his displeasure clearly. He soon realized his strategy had backfired and called a meeting with the dean to clarify his discontent with her performance.

Relieved to know that her boss was not incompetent, just a poor communicator, she immediately began working on a performance improvement plan. It did not take long before she was earning full merit pay.

Sensitivity Conceals Truth

As people are drawn together in the workplace, their beliefs, values, and practices are bound to create differing opinions and attitudes. Keeping silent about these differences as though they do not exist—adding them to the list of unresolved issues—erects artificial barriers, stifles fruitful dialogue, and drives well-intentioned people apart.

The longer the list, the more tense and anxious people will become. An effective way to get these unmentionable topics on the table is to gather people together on a regular basis to resolve those issues on the list.

Begin by asking each participant to anonymously write down on 3 x 5 index cards those issues he or she would like to see resolved. Compile a master list and then have each person rank the issues in the order they are ready to discuss. Next, work through the list together one item at a time beginning with the lowest priority. Schedule the first session for about ninety minutes in order to give the participants ample time to learn how the process works.

The heaviest, more serious issues top the list. Heaviest meaning an issue so sensitive that no one has dared mention it for fear of what might happen. Such unresolved issues have been on the list so long that they take on additional weight and unwarranted significance.

It is best to start at the bottom of the list with the least sensitive issues and save the heavier issues for later. This process often exposes those in opposition to the possibility that they may not "know the truth" and that they may not be able to uncover the facts without help from their peers.

As potential Doers work their way through the unresolved issues list, they learn how to express their concerns without prejudice or judgment, how to ask difficult questions, and how to bring up the issues that are keeping them collaborating with their coworkers.

When a festering issue is liable to pit one person against another, consider using an outside facilitator who is not involved and has no personal interest in the outcome.

Here is an example of how a facilitator helped to resolve a longstanding feud between two critical care nurses in a large metropolitan hospital.

According to the Director, the discord started when nurse Swanson supposedly complained that she did not want nurse Martin taking care of her mother who was a patient at that time.

The implication from Swanson was that Martin was incompetent; at least that is how Martin perceived it. Over the ensuing months that the conflict dragged on, the rumormongers had embellished the story, adding unfounded tidbits that inflamed the situation.

The truth came out when the two antagonists were brought together and surrounded by a caring team of colleagues. Swanson's objection was not a question of Martin's competency, but rather one of averting a conflict.

Swanson was concerned that her overly critical mother would pose a problem for Martin who was known and admired for her soft spoken and caring nature. Even though Swanson admired Martin for her gentleness, she felt it was not a good match for her mother.

Swanson was actually concerned that Martin would be overpowered by her mother and wanted to spare her colleague, who she regarded highly, from a potentially negative experience. Once both parties recognized the truth, they sort forgiveness and agreed to communicate honestly in the future.

No one enjoys working in a tension-filled environment. Research on employee turnover shows that the Doers are the first to flee a stress-producing workplace. Consider what it would mean, then, should your best people leave to seek peace elsewhere; you would be surrounded by overly sensitive underachievers.

The Upward Voice

Research shows that the primary reason chief executives fail is not from a lack of skills or abilities, but rather from not being aware of information that could negatively impact their organization.

Seniors executives need to hear the voice of truth from those closet to the problem who deal with the customers and thus in the best position to recommend solutions.

The Upward Voice refers to communications directed to someone in the organization's hierarchy with the authority to take action. Moving information up the chain of command begins by the formation of problem solving teams consisting of representatives from all organizational levels that are known to be reliable and trustworthy.

In order for The Upward Voice to be loud enough to be heard when it reaches the top level decision makers, lower level participants must first be assured that they are not putting themselves at risk of retaliation for speaking out and that they are not wasting their time voicing their concerns and proposing solutions.

Without The Upward Voice in place to clarify expectations and neutralize negativity an organization is opening the door to frequent communications calamities between the upper and lower levels. Just such a situation is illustrated by the following true story:

Picture a small city run by a city manager serving at the discretion of an elected city council. According to the local newspaper, expenditures were getting out of hand, and the council was under pressure to monitor the budget more closely. Adding fuel to the fire was the adverse community reaction to a recent round of pay raises for the city manager and the department heads.

The city manager was under pressure by the council to justify the salaries of his department heads. After discussing various options including the freezing of all salaries, the council recommended that department heads get out into the community more so that the voters would see who runs the city.

Later that day the city manager verbally passed on that recommendation to the department heads. Hearing what he thought was a mandate the public works director and the maintenance superintendent spent that afternoon driving around the city.

Very early the next morning the superintendent met with the trash and recycle collection crews as they were warming up their trucks and told them that instead of making their rounds as usual, they would be trimming mistletoe from the trees in the parks. Trash collection would have to wait.

It was not long after that the city hall receptionist was flooded with complaints about the trash and recycle bins being left at the curbside. The city manager and the public works director tracked down the superintendent, who was surprised by their anger and accusations.

He explained that during their drive around the city, the public works director had told him that the council wanted some action to justify the recent pay raises. Since the only thing the director had commented on during their trip was the overgrowth of the mistletoe in the city parks, the superintendent assumed it to be a priority.

The city council, in a mood to fire everyone connected with the fiasco, called an emergency meeting. As the meeting progressed it became clear that the council members were stunned to learn that their suggestion to "get out in the community more" had used as the reason to halt the trash and recycle pickup.

All they had intended was for those who worked for the city to have higher community visibility. They envisioned appearances at Chamber of Commerce functions, speeches to the downtown association, presentations to service clubs and schools, and interviews on local TV and radio stations. In other words, the council expected the department heads to mingle with the citizens and promote the council's vision of the city's future.

The city manager perceived their directive differently. He thought that the council was upset with his "overpaid" department heads for not earning their keep. His strategy was to light a fire under them before he lost his job. The public works director, in turn, viewed the request as additional work for him. If there were infrastructure problems somewhere in the city, he had better find them quickly and set about to fix them. After all, he was close to retirement and did not want anything to mess that up.

The superintendent simply thought the director was mad at him for something. This made him very uncomfortable and eager to get back on his boss' good side by attending to whatever was bugging him. The pickup crews knew something was screwy, but kept their opinions to themselves and did what they were told without question.

As the real story unfolded the players began to see, perhaps for the first time, that their communications channels were badly clogged. At first they were disappointed and disillusioned by the discovery. But, with a little push, they revisited some of their past misadventures. The trip was worthwhile, for it made them realize just how poorly they had been communicating their intentions from one level to the next. The council agreed to work with the city manager and the department heads to find better ways of communicating their intentions.

Soon thereafter, encouraged by their eagerness to improve communications, the management team set about to create The Upward Voice. It did not take long for the supervisors and staff to get on board. Gradually, as other citizens were drawn into the process of assessing the level of services and recommending changes, the atmosphere of tension and suspicion was replaced by one of anticipation and cooperation. All municipalities struggle to match budget limitations with citizens' expectations, but this city learned how to use The Upward Voice to make that struggle pay off.

Establishing the Upward Voice

Phase 1 — Climate Setting: Management calls the meeting and provides assurance that no reprimands will be given to anyone who voices complaints or shares negative information.

Phase 2 — Information Collecting: Doers form topic-teams to list those variances or blockages that are hampering organizational performance and productivity.

Phase 3 — Information Sharing: Management reviews the lists from each topic-team. A spokesperson may be assigned to help clarify topic-team statements.

Phase 4 — Priority Setting: Management and topic-teams rank order those items that need further exploration. Topic-teams come back with suggestions for action.

Phase 5 — Action Planning: Management and topic-teams each make a list of what they will take action on, including timetables and resource allocations.

Phase 6 — Follow-up: Management and topic-teams meet to develop action plans based on commitments made in Phase 5. The results are reported in Phase 7.

Phase 7 — Progress Review: All participants reconvene regularly to report progress, settle disputes, develop plans, and share emerging issues.

Successful organizations like the one in the story above have come to understand and appreciate the benefits of having Doers join in The Upward Voice. Positive outcomes include increased open communications, disclosure of personal and departmental conflicts, improved leader/follower relations, and higher levels of productivity from non-performers and underachievers.

Chapter 4 – Direction

In a fast-paced, loosely structured organization, planning tends to be a bothersome task. If a written plan does exist, it was probably pieced together at a recent management retreat and is gathering dust on a shelf alongside plans from previous years. One by one, each well-intentioned strategy died a quiet death, drowned in a sea of unforeseen events.

One way to determine how well the direction of a company is understood by those who do the work is to bring in an outside facilitator to meet with employees in small groups. This process can reveal how followers feel about the direction their leaders are going.

It is from such gatherings that the subject of direction setting can be discussed. The facilitator will ask a series of probing questions, which the respondents answer by raising their hands or speaking out.

Here is one example, "How many of you do not need a boss to tell you how to do your job?" The majority of hands go up.

This is quickly followed by: "How many did not raise your hand because you were afraid your boss would find out?" Additional hands are raised.

Next question, "Based on the large showing of hands, it is obvious that you do not need a boss. Is that correct?" A resounding "No!" quickly follows.

Finally query: "Well, if you know what to do without being told, then why do you need a boss? Their response comes quickly and loudly, "To give us direction."

So, what happens if your boss fails to provide direction? Like your Doer counterparts, you yourself must continue to move ahead and keep pace with the prevailing winds of change. To keep your crew on course, you must show them how to respond faster, reduce costs, improve efficiency, and adjust to change. If those charged with planning and directing your organization are not providing direction, then it may be up to you and others at your level to find a way to get ahead on your own.

Doers are continuously frustrated by the lack of direction from leaders who do not look to the future, focusing instead on immediate results and quick fixes. If that sounds familiar, stay tuned, this chapter will provide some welcome relief and some helpful suggestions.

SHIFTING FOCUS

In preceding chapters the focus has been on dysfunction in those around and below you. It is time to shift the focus to those who influence you from above. If you accept that there have always been dysfunctional people in organizations, it stands to reason that some of them have "floated" to the top.

Despite the lack of attention paid to dysfunction in management literature, there have always been dysfunctional people in our organizations, at all levels— from the highest levels of senior management to the lowliest subordinate. Their individual level of dysfunction, combined with their level of power within the organization, determines the impact their behavior may have upon it— and the impact you can have upon their behavior.

Coping with a dysfunctional boss is far more difficult than working with a dysfunctional subordinate. The impact of each on the organization is also very different. Dysfunction at the subordinate level impacts production, customer service, quality, materials, waste, turnover, safety, and absenteeism. These are all performance-based characteristics that are measurable and easily changed, once an agreement is reached to do so.

Dysfunction at the top takes on more sinister, undesirable forms like favoritism, racism, sexism, nepotism, cronyism, and ageism. These organizational characteristics affect values and culture. They defy measurement and are difficult to change from below.

At the higher levels, dysfunction is less about performance and more about power. Functional executives use their power to move things along, to overcome obstacles and resistance to changes, and get the job done right. They focus on organizational performance through personal achievement.

In contrast, dysfunctional seniors use their power to keep things from happening while they figure out how to take the credit should something work or how to avoid responsibility should it fail. Putting previously agreed upon actions on hold is a telltale sign of a dysfunctional decision maker. Overriding the recommendations of subordinates and making arbitrary decisions with no explanation are additional signs of a dysfunctional boss.

The life of an organization, its principles, ethics, style, values, and morality, are shaped by the actions of those at the top. Executives, who hire their friends and relatives, overlook minorities, promote incompetent subordinates, and contract with suppliers who return favors are shaping a dysfunctional culture. Yet it would be difficult to get them to admit that such actions are demoralizing.

You may be wondering how such dysfunctional managers reach the top of their organizations? You should also be concerned that it does not happen to you on the way up. As we get into the reasons behind such behavior, it might be helpful to keep in mind that these are not bad people they are just incompetent as managers.

Some are victims of the Peter Principle, which says that organizations tend to promote people until they reach their level of incompetence. After that, they supposedly cannot go any higher, that is, unless they have made friends with those higher up. In that case, they will continue moving up the ladder, because the old adage is true: it is not *what* they know, but *who* they know that counts.

Not all dysfunctional executives reached the higher levels with help from their friends. Some got there in legitimate and laudable ways, earning their advancement through hard work and sacrifice. But now that they have reached the top, they are burned out. They want to rest on their laurels. They have already "given it their best shot" and have no more to give.

Then there are those mentally gifted managers who were promoted because of their special knowledge and technical competence. Unfortunately, their unique skills have since become commonplace and they are no longer needed, but they are unaware of it. Managers like this are stuck at a level of *unconscious incompetence*. In other words, "they don't know what they don't know, and they probably don't care." They got theirs; why should they work any harder?

It is also important to realize that *you* may have contributed to the dysfunction at the top of your workplace. How so you might ask? By withholding comments, criticisms, or concerns from those above or by adding your own twist to information as it wends its way upward. This has become such a common practice that folks make a joke of it.

Perhaps it is funny, but it is also a sad commentary on life at the upper level. Whoever said "It's lonely at the top," must have been an executive in a directionless workplace. If the bosses are setting their own course and steering the ship based on contaminated information from below, it is not totally their fault if the ship runs aground.

Information Flow

Comparing the flow of information in functional and dysfunctional organizations is like looking at an hourglass. An hourglass is a device to measure time by the flow of sand between the upper and lower chambers. A narrow opening between the upper and lower chambers controls the flow.

Imagine the hourglass as your organization, with the sand representing information flowing from the upper level into the lower level.

What would happen if the information flow were inverted? In other words, what is the potential for information sharing? When the hourglass is standing upright information flows freely between the upper and lower chambers then you are in a functional organization that values planning.

If, however, the hourglass is lying on its side information settles at either end, then your organization is probably dysfunctional. The people at either end know what they know, but there is no flow between them. Planning, if there is any, is conducted independently in isolation.

The middle level of a functional organization is always under pressure as the information comes down from above and then rebounds from below. The good news for Doers in a functional setting is that even if the information flows under pressure, they can count on it to contain realistic time lines, reasonable goals, established priorities, measurable expectations, and a clear direction to follow.

Frustration derived from the lack of information flow is usually very high in a dysfunctional organization. Upper level pressure moves downward in the form of directives, deadlines, and disciplinary action. Pressure from the lower chamber floats upward in the form of complaints, challenges, and concerns. In general, Doers in the middle of the hourglass know very little, but are expected to do a lot, which is one of the reasons they suffer.

If you identify with the latter description, then you probably feel that your hands are tied and there is nothing you can do. Such is not the case. If you sincerely want to make a meaningful difference, you can. Later in this chapter you will find out how.

There is very little interest in formulating plans in a dysfunctional organization. Until the organization determines why it exists, what it has to offer, who it wishes to serve, and what it hopes to achieve, leaders and followers will carry on as usual.

Rather than wait for this to happen you can develop your own action plan that will provide those within your sphere of influence with the direction they seek.

Time Management

A few years back there was a big push to better manage time. Management seminars and books promoted the idea that if you tried harder you could manage your time better. Most people attending the seminars were sent there by a boss who, according to the participants, was the one who was wasting their time. It was not long before the participants could see a connection between the inefficient use of time and their incompetent boss.

As time management technologies were adapted, Doer efficiency increased. Unfortunately, the technology had the opposite effect on management. The implementation of these innovations uncovered their lack of planning skills and their inability to cope with shorter time frames and multiple priorities.

As consumer scrutiny, economic uncertainty, and technological advances continue, upper level management is finding it increasingly more difficult to keep up. To overcome this deficiency in your work setting, you should consider taking on the responsibility for moving an idea through the stages of planning, research, development, production, and distribution. The Planning Wheel described below and depicted in Figure 4 provides a way for Doers like you to make up for the lack of direction.

Direction Setting

As decision makers are finding it increasingly more difficult to keep pace with an ever-changing market, those charged with providing direction claim that things are changing so fast that a formal plan would be out of date before it could be implemented.

An organization without a plan or at least a planning process is not likely to update its vision, mission, goals and objectives either. Which means that there is no reliable method for Doers to establish and meet performance expectations other than by gut feeling.

If management merely relies on the winds of fate as their guide, they are more likely to run the ship aground. Until that happens, Doers can at least plot a course that accommodates the ever-changing currents in their area of responsibility.

An interactive process, like The Planning Wheel, provides direction and determines your future actions. Once a plan is published, your purpose is made known to all those with whom you work.

Without a clearly understood and accepted purpose, it is easy to lose the sense of direction. You become confused about what the future holds. The same goes for those whose lead you follow, the coworkers who struggle alongside you, and anyone who looks to you for guidance and direction.

The primary reason for making your purpose known is to establish a baseline of expectations that has meaning and can be measured. Doers know that the true challenge of direction setting is to understand that they cannot change something without first knowing its purpose. Once a purpose is defined, it becomes a matter of harnessing the energy of external pressures to work your way through the uncharted waters the lie ahead.

As you ponder how best to apply the Planning Wheel to your area of responsibility, think first about how you would complete this statement:

The purpose of the unit, section, department, branch, or organization where I work is to _____.

If your response came quickly, can be explained easily, and fills you with hope, then you are working in a purpose-driven workplace where the direction is clear and the future holds promise. The Planning Wheel will help you to stay focused as you move competently and confidently toward the challenges that lie ahead.

If your response was slow in coming, is difficult to express, and leaves you confused, you are working in a personality-driven workplace where the direction is obscure and the future harbors doubt. The Planning Wheel provides the tools you will need to close the gap between where you are and where you want to be.

The Planning Wheel

The Planning Wheel is a contemporary model resembling a ship's steering wheel, which controls the rudder, and therefore, the direction of the ship. At the center of the wheel is the hub, representing the purpose of the "voyage." Radiating outward from the hub are the spokes representing communication channels, connecting the hub with the rim of the wheel. At the intersection of each spoke and the rim lies a point of action representing an opportunity for your team— your crew— to receive direction and report their observations.

Before we look at the points of the Planning Wheel, it would be helpful to understand why someone at your level should be interested in planning. Because when you want to step into a leadership role, you will need to know how to do it yourself. It could improve your chances of moving higher up where you could really make a difference.

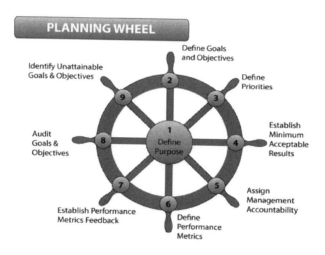

Figure 4 — Planning Wheel

Define Purpose

Defining a purpose is the most critical part of a successful planning strategy. A clearly defined purpose statement tells the world why you exist, what you have to offer, who you wish to serve, and what you hope to achieve. Without it, much time, talent, and treasure will be wasted while coworkers do their own thing. To be effective, the planning strategy should provide your team with a vision and a sense of direction, while at the same time remaining flexible and responsive to the challenge of change.

Define Goals & Objectives

Goals and objectives define the amount of work or number of tasks your team is expected to complete, the time they need to spend doing it, the degree of accuracy they need to maintain, and the manner in which they should conduct themselves as they perform. Goals state what the target is and how often they are expected to hit it. Objectives provide individual direction aligned with the organization's direction.

Define Priorities

Prioritizing establishes the importance of each goal and objective. It determines the order in which specific actions need to be taken. When resources are short and deadlines are pressing, a set of well-defined priorities enables Doers to decide which goals matter and which can be set aside temporarily. Attaching priorities empowers your team to calculate the cost-benefit of alternate actions. Thus informed, they can react to change quickly and smoothly by shifting priorities or setting new goals and objectives.

Establish Minimum Acceptable Results

Without a set of standards your team is likely to let some vital tasks go while they focus on the higher priorities. Failure to maintain minimum standards for each task is the primary source of bottlenecks, production stoppages, and work slowdowns. Knowing how to balance their efforts between minimum results and high priorities is vital to your team's ability to achieve their goals and objectives.

Assign Management Accountability

One way to expedite accountability is to submit your carefully crafted plan to your boss with the stipulation that unless you are directed otherwise you intend to move forward. The longer he or she ponders the issue of liability, the more time you have to prove the worthiness of your ideas. Once your boss sees the positive results, he is bound to step forward and make himself accountable. After that, you are in a position to accept accountability if you know what will work, or delegate it upward to management if you need more time to test your ideas.

Define Performance Metrics

Knowing what to focus on is the key to getting the results you expect. Doers need to know how much time, talent, and treasure it will take to meet each performance goal. Also, they will want to know which indicators will be used to measure their performance. Hard indicators, such as budget, quotas, errors, profits, sales, expenses, and deadlines, can be applied to measure efficiency. Soft indicators, such as satisfaction, experience, confidence, attitude, values, spirit, and motivation, typically measure effectiveness.

Establish Performance Metrics Feedback

Your team members want to know how they are doing. They are particularly interested in finding out when they are not meeting their performance objectives. To have meaning, feedback must be fair, objective, and timely. One way to ensure fairness is to involve participant observers. If the report contains observations from coworkers, customers, suppliers, and employees in other departments, in addition to the supervisor, it would cover "360 degrees" and provide an objective view.

Audit Goals & Objectives

A review of performance expectations should point out which goals and objectives were difficult to achieve and which were relatively easy. This is also a good time to uncover any negative side effects resulting from goal ambiguity or goal conflicts. Some team members may be stressed out from overload, while others may need greater challenges. Provide recognition to those who met or exceeded their targets. Prepare corrective action plans for those with results lower that expected.

Identify Unattainable Goals & Objectives

Take a close look at what is not working and try to decide what can be done to change the outcome. Pull your team together and discuss which goals and objectives are a waste of their time and energies. Decide whether these goals are worth any further investment. If attainment of a goal is still important, identify the constraints that are blocking success and find ways to remove these barriers or lessen the impact they are having on production.

Confirming The Purpose

Now that you understand how to work the Planning Wheel, you can think of yourself not only as a Doer, but also as a planner. You may not be the one developing the original plan, but you are able to fill in the blanks if those higher up leave anything out.

By the time you have worked your way around the Planning Wheel, the organization's purpose or your part in it may have altered slightly or even changed radically, depending upon the winds of fate. If your purpose has changed, you may need to cease working on some goals and objectives and begin anew on others.

This is the best time to make a mid-course correction. By letting go of nonproductive activities, you can make room for new ones that better fit the revised purpose. Even if the purpose has not changed, it makes no sense to continue working on goals and objectives that are nonproductive. Your team will appreciate knowing that you are willing to let go of a goal when there is no reason to pursue it any further.

The action points around the rim of the Planning Wheel provide for the constant exchange and review of information. This two-way, interactive system is what gives the Planning Wheel its dynamic flexibility. It allows the purpose to be reassessed in response to change.

The planning wheel can be entered from any point on the rim. For instance, if you were assigned to a new team, you might plug in at Stage 8 by looking at the current goals and objectives. If they do exist, then you can assess how well they are being performed and support the continuation of the work processes currently in place. If there are no stated goals and objectives or those that do exist are outdated then you can enter at Stage 1 or 2.

As the new person it is important for you to make a good first impression. Gathering the new team around the Planning Wheel is a great way to establish yourself as a Doer and to improve the outcome simultaneously.

Whenever a job is not being done well or the team does not feel good about doing it, they are probably doing something outside the scope of their purpose. Unless they have a clearly defined purpose, it is easy to get caught up in doing unproductive things.

Discoveries like this are not likely to be known at the upper levels. By understanding where you and the other Doers fit into the plan, you are now in possession of information that can be useful to those higher up. (See Upward Voice in Chapter 3.)

Chapter 5 — Collaboration

Our education system teaches students to compete against each other for recognition and rewards. Having been taught collectively and tested individually throughout their formative years, graduates find the transition from learning to earning difficult because the teaching and testing processes are reversed.

First-time job placements enter the workforce valuing only what they can do for themselves or can accomplish on their own. Sharing what they know with another student was considered cheating and those who were caught collaborating suffered negative consequences.

Adhering to the education and socialization model they followed in school, young people, in an effort to be accepted, tend to join cliques made up of people who look, think, speak, and act like them.

Cliques are like miniature societies with mindsets of their own. When the goals of a clique are not in alignment with those of other work units, performance and productivity decline. If left unchecked, an organization can become dysfunctional simply because its workforce lacks the confidence, ability, and desire to work together.

Here is how one frustrated CEO broke up the self-serving cliques that were dominating his company and reassembled them into collaborative work units.

Ron was fed up with the destructive competition between his production crews. Cliques of mostly new hires, who thought it was clever to sabotage the "old timers," were disrupting the workflow at several key assembly stations.

Many of the Doers, who had held things together in the past, were either gone or getting ready to leave. If Ron were going to turn things around, he would need to rally the remaining Doers and give them the authority to lead the charge for change.

In desperation, Ron called the department heads together in the conference room and posted the names of every supervisor together with a ranking calculated from their past performance reviews. After explaining his intention to break up the existing cliques, he directed them to pick new supervisors in an NFL-like draft. Realizing the stakes were high, the department heads made certain to pick one of the Doers still on the list each time their turn came around. Any supervisor not selected was assumed to be a non-performer or underachievers and was given the choice of demotion to line worker or resignation.

Those supervisors picked in the draft were immediately enrolled in an extensive Performance Management and Process Improvement training program. This seemingly bizarre strategy rapidly rejuvenated the workforce by instilling a collaborative spirit throughout the company.

Peer Coaching

Remember how nerve-wracking it was the first time you were hired or moved into a new position? In the beginning, you had no sense of place. You probably felt a little alienated and lost. After a while, if nobody gave you guidance or support, you began to wonder if you made the right decision. The longer the uncertainty was, the less confidence you had in yourself and in your work.

Like the fellow in the story that follows the type of welcome you received was a big factor in determining how you as a new hire felt about being part of the team.

Earl, for example, had accepted a position working for a biotech company reported to be on a fast track. He had high expectations for what he could contribute to the company. By the time he had been there a week, though, no one had spoken to him about the goals of his department or the immediate objectives of his job. He had only a vague idea of the projects he would be working on.

When he asked a coworker about the project folders on his desk, he was told, "You're the genius, you figure it out." A short time later, Earl received an accusatory email from his team leader complaining about his missing an important deadline; one he had never heard about.

Earl had the uncomfortable feeling of being out of place. No one seemed to notice that he was around. The fact that he was new seemed to count against him. Not being there for very long implied that he either did not know anything or that he had nothing of value to offer. Sink or swim—it was up to him. Ultimately, he sank.

Contrast Earl's experience with that of Amy's. Like Earl, she entered her new position with high expectations and a little apprehension about where she would fit in. Her doubts were quickly dispelled after her peer coach spent an entire afternoon explaining her duties and letting her know about department goals and objectives. Later, she took Amy around to meet the other members of her team who seemed to know a great deal about her background. Her welcome was sincere.

Amy was soon working on tasks that were both fulfilling and meaningful. She went home at the end of the second week knowing she was a valued member of her team.

What Amy's coworkers did right was to show her the respect due a new team member. They told her what her job was and showed how what she did contributed to the team's goals. They introduced her to those she would be working with in other units, which made her feel complete. In other words, the team was assembled around her.

Rather than respect Earl's skills and abilities, his coworkers made him feel like a stranger. There was no recognition of his place on the team. The people around him were working independently at cross-purposes and not accomplishing very much. Rather than pulling together as a team, Earl's coworkers were pulling themselves apart. Instead of looking forward to a prosperous future, Earl was looking for a way out.

The difference between Amy's fruitful journey and Earl's wasteful venture is in how well peer coaches help new hires to fit in fast and to find job satisfaction quickly. Amy's colleagues did it right and Earl's did it wrong.

Doers have the skills necessary to excel in whatever job they may be assigned. By empowering them to pass along these skills as peer coaches, an organization is able to replace the *me-ness* that promotes individualism with a *we-ness* that fosters collaboration.

Unintended Consequences

Taking on the role of a peer coach can be a challenge. It can also be very rewarding as you watch your colleagues gain in their proficiency and ability to solve problems quickly and collaboratively. Keep in mind, however, that those most in need of your guidance are the least willing to tackle a problem unless they are confident of a positive result. They view problem solving as a high-risk situation that could get them in trouble or even jeopardize their jobs. So, tread carefully and be patient.

Unlike Doers who seek opportunities to make a positive difference, these status quo seekers maintain a low profile and show little initiative. If they do take on a problem, they want to be left alone to resolve it in a way that makes sense to them. Any pressure to meet deadlines or provide feedback is liable to be greeted with a scowl and a caustic refrain like "Quit breathing down my neck," or "Get off my back." Acting alone without consultation or collaboration is the root cause of most unintended consequences.

Problem Solving

When you set out to resolve problems that are outside your sphere of influence, there is often no clear place to start. Unless a particular situation is begging for your attention, start by making a list of outcomes where the results failed to meet expectations.

Use the four-step, problem-solving guide as your template, filling in each section as the details emerge. Resist the urge to solve the problem until the investigation is complete.

Step I – Identify Cause
1. Define precisely what went wrong.
2. Gather data on what, where, when, and how it happened.
3. Explore the factors that might have triggered the deviation.
4. Select the most likely cause for the deviation.
5. Test assumptions—is the problem likely to reoccur?

Step II – Develop Options
1. Determine who "owns" the problem.
2. Define expected desired results.
3. Generate a list of workable options in priority order.
4. Invite input from those impacted by the alternatives.
5. Pick the solution most likely to work.

Step III – Implement Solution
1. Seek out possible opposition to the action plan.
2. Brainstorm potential threats to the decision.
3. Determine the severity of each threat.
4. Estimate the probability of a negative outcome.
5. Clarify authority, responsibility, and reporting relationships.

Step IV – Evaluate Result
1. Set timelines and measurements.
2. Establish negative and positive incentives for compliance.
3. Make sure that appropriate action was taken.
4. Follow-up to see if the problem was resolved.
5. Record the results.

The following examples are meant to get you started:

- In an effort to boost morale, management decided to form a company baseball team. The person assigned to order equipment was unfamiliar with the game. He correctly assumed that most players were right-handed, but wrongly concluded that they would catch the ball with a glove worn on that hand. The team was shocked and surprised when a shipment of left-handed catchers mitts arrived.

- A produce clerk, unfamiliar with the avocado and uncertain what perishable meant, stored a newly arrived shipment in the freezer. Responding to the newspaper ad touting the many qualities of this delicious fruit, customers quickly bought out the lot. Just as quickly, they returned their purchases, disgusted by the blackened pulp they had discovered when they sliced through the skin.

- A newly installed automated payroll system incorrectly treated a year-end bonus as a pay raise. This error pushed many employees into a higher tax bracket, triggering a deduction of back payroll taxes for the entire year from their next paycheck. Employees were astounded to receive $0.00 pay because the amount deducted was more than their bimonthly earnings. The direct deposit system was also thrown into chaos because it could not cope with zero as an amount.

As you develop your own list of unintended consequences, you might find it helpful to look ahead to the *Dysfunctional Behaviors Checklist* in Chapter 9.

Team Formation

The purpose in forming an organization is to create a place where individuals achieve collectively what they cannot accomplish alone. According to Christopher Avery, author of *Teamwork Is An Individual Skill*, "Becoming skilled at doing more with others may be the single most important thing you can do to increase your value—regardless of your level of authority."

Pulling individuals together to form a team is much like constructing a sand castle on the beach. When a high tide comes in, a portion of the castle may be washed away and need rebuilding. A rogue wave could knock down the whole structure and leave only a trace outline of what was once there. Continually forming and reforming is the challenge peer coaches have to face, which is why it is called team*work*.

Overcoming this challenge will require the application of a new ideology—a set of factors upon which team members can get to know and trust one another by working together on the same tasks at the same time. The guiding principles that help to form task-oriented relationships set forth in Chapter 1: Relationships can also be used to prepare aspiring Doers for collaboration.

Once relationships begin to form, all that is needed is a way to pull isolated individuals together around a common task. Fortunately, a very practical, easy-to-use process known as Responsibility Charting is available. In the following section, you will learn how to enhance your effectiveness as a peer coach by introducing this process throughout your sphere of influence.

Responsibility Charting

The best way to understand Responsibility Charting is to pick a case from your list of unintended consequences. Then, note the various tasks each of the folks involved in the case should have undertaken and the order in which each task should have been completed. Now, visualize each person with a blank space beside his or her name in which to place a letter representing one of the roles and responsibilities explained below and depicted in Figure 5.

RESPONSIBILITY CHARTING

	Tina	Armond	Bailey	Mason	Skyler	
Task #1	C	R	A	I	I	
Task #2	I	C	A	I	R	
Task #3	R	I	A	I	C	
Task #4	I	C	A	R	I	
Task #5						
Task #6						

C - Consult The person(s) to be consulted when the action is being taken.
I - Inform The person(s) to be informed when the action is complete.

Taken from: Designing Complex Organizations by Jay R. Galbreath.

Figure 5 — Responsibility Charting

Roles And Responsibilities

[R]-Identifies the person responsible for completing the task. This is the person accountable for taking action. As a general rule, there will only be one [R] for each task. The person selected needs to understand and accept the performance expectations such as the budget, timelines, production standards, and any other factors that are critical to the successful completion of this task.

[A]-Identifies the person whose approval is needed before action is taken. This makes it clear to the person assigned the [R] that he/she needs to confer with someone higher up the chain of command with authority before taking action. The [R] will also need to check with whomever is assigned the [A] to determine just how far he/she can go before providing additional feedback on what has been accomplished.

[C]-Indicates those with whom a consultation is required or recommended. Assigning one or more [C]s to the task makes it clear the [R] will not be working alone. The [C]s need to know how much time, talent, and treasure they are expected to contribute, this is best accomplished while the [R] and [A] are present. After the resources are approved, only the [R] and the [C]s need to attend future task meetings—a time saver for everyone.

[I]- Identifies those who need to be informed through status updates from the [R] as the task progresses. The [I]s are just receiving information and not held responsible for picking up the slack if the [R] falls behind or fails to perform as planned. Also, the [I]s do not need to attend future task meetings because the person assigned the [R] will keep them informed— another time saving feature.

Armed with the knowledge of how to rectify the unintended consequences on your list, you are now in a position to share your findings with those involved. Walking them through the Responsibility Charting process will demonstrate how each of them would have been better off collaborating and communicating with other coworkers who had the information and expertise necessary to produce the desired outcome.

Alternative Applications

Responsibility Charting is a dynamic productivity tool that has many uses. For example, a government agency with a reputation for substandard performance was assigned a new director who was determined to turn things around. A productivity study disclosed that the average staff person spent nearly 40 percent of each day in meetings trying to correct inaccuracies created by people from other departments. Much of the meeting time was spent shifting blame, finding fault, and pointing fingers at others who could not explain or defend their actions because they were not in attendance.

The director made a bold decision to suspend all staff meetings and directed them instead to use Responsibility Charting to define, align, and assign roles, relationships and responsibilities before any action was taken.

It was not long before the entire staff stopped wasting time trying to figure out who was supposed to do what and instead enjoyed a fruitful period of high performance teamwork. Within 18 months they raised their statewide ranking among 58 comparative agencies from 53rd to 1st and received national recognition for their achievement.

In addition to defining who is on the team and what task he or she is to perform, Responsibility Charting helps keep track of the status of each task. It can also be used to evaluate team member contributions to each stated outcome. For example, someone who has performed well in a consulting [C] role on several tasks could be ready to assume full responsibility [R] on a task that is coming up. This is a good way to train potential Doers to accept more responsibility and to get them to appreciate the benefits of collaboration.

Because Responsibility Charting provides the structure for building teams, it is very helpful when launching a new venture or getting a derailed project back on track. Gathering those involved in a project to chart each task, can clear up misunderstandings, misinformation, and miscommunication. Responsibility Charting is truly a marvelous tool in its simplicity and effectiveness.

Organizations with multiple work sites typically set up an automated system of digital charts so that project leaders can assemble a virtual team without ever having the members meet in person. Instead, they gather on-line in chat rooms to discuss tasks, seek consultation, and keep each other informed.

This virtual, exacting style is useful in larger, more complex systems where records are necessary and people may not be available to meet face to face. However, smaller organizations often prefer a simpler, less formal version.

Instead of letter designations, "hats" are used to verbally indicate who is performing in what role on any given task. For example, you might be in the middle of discussing a sticky situation with your colleagues when someone asks, "What would you do?"

As they listen to your reply, some may interpret what you say as a directive because they see you as a peer coach wearing an authority [A] "hat." Your reputation as a Doer may leave some with the impression that you are wearing the responsibility [R] "hat." Others may see you wearing the information [I] or consultation [C] "hat" and figure you are just offering advice. Lack of clarity in situations like this creates ambiguity and role confusion, which are the building blocks of organizational dysfunction.

Until people get used to the charting process, the best way to prevent role confusion is to declare what "hat" you are wearing each time you offer input or answer questions. Let those you are coaching know that if they do get confused, it is okay to ask for clarification. What is not okay is guessing or assuming, which just leads to more unintended consequences.

Responsibility Charting empowers low performers by infusing them with new energy and clarity of purpose. As they focus more on their responsibilities, they will come to rely on each other when they are confused. Now that you know how to apply this multi-use tool, you will find that many of those folks who were previously known to be under-performers are ready to accept responsibility for getting it right. A more equitable distribution of work tasks will bring a greater level of collaboration, which ultimately leads to higher performance and greater productivity.

Gaining Acceptance

Managers in today's complex organizations are discovering that getting staff together to develop a common set of goals is not only difficult, but it is frequently divisive and disruptive to the normal work flow. Their challenge is to meld the individual perceptions and expectations into a unified vision.

The primary obstacles keeping employees from coming to a common understanding are most often the variances that exist between their attitudes and their behaviors. For example, Doers willingly share their viewpoints and eagerly discuss ideas with others. Not so for underachievers, who are suspicious of open deliberations. They either keep quiet or do not respond wholeheartedly and truthfully in communal settings. Getting these under-performers to accept their share of responsibility then becomes a stumbling block.

When it comes to accountability, there are two types of employees: those who accept it and those who avoid it. Earlier in this chapter, we introduced Responsibility Charting as a way of tracking who is taking responsibility and who is not. Most likely it is the underachievers who are shirking responsibility. If you let them, the Doers will take on more responsibility because they thrive on it. Meanwhile the underachievers sit back and enjoy the benefits of someone else's labor, thus splitting the group apart even further.

As these and other behavioral differences are uncovered, some managers simply lay the blame on the non-performers and try to have them replaced. But ridding the organization of nonfunctional people, even if it were possible, is not the answer. A better solution is to learn how to work them.

First, it is important to try to understand some of the underlying reasons for their behavior. Beginning with childhood, underachievers have been surrounded by authority figures constantly pointing out their faults. Thus, even a well-intentioned exploration of a problem will arouse their instinctive fear of being punished. They suspect that any group assembly is really a disguised attempt to fix the blame and to humiliate those at fault, in which case they will strongly resist self-disclosure in public. Before underachievers participate willingly in the information sharing process, they need to appreciate the benefits of mutual discovery.

The more you study workplace behavior, the more you understand why underachievers have negative feelings toward group processes. Group decision-making reminds them of the dreaded school ground ritual known as choosing sides. As children, they would give up the chance to join in the game rather than run the risk of not being picked. The same is true when they enter the work force. Fear of rejection is stronger than their desire to participate.

The opposite is true for Doers, for whom the opportunity to be part of the group outweighs the risk of rejection. If one group does not want them, they find another that does. Doers view groups as positive places for learning about themselves and others. They view peer feedback as one of the benefits of group membership. Doers purposely explore relationships to discover how others perceive them. If the group's view is negative, they either work on self-improvement to be accepted or find another group that appreciates them for who they are and what they bring to the relationship.

Clearly, the gap between these two different employee types is widening. The rising pressure on employees to do more with less will spread the gap even further in the coming years. Closing that gap is a management responsibility. Spotting it is easy, though, if you know what to look for; it is simply a matter of observing people in action. Next time your group meets, shift the facilitation responsibility to someone else and focus on how each person provides input and gives feedback. The most noteworthy attitudinal and behavioral differences between high and low performers in groups are described below.

The Group Acceptance Pact

Mainstream management methods can only bridge the gap between functional and dysfunctional employees, bridging, at best, merely provides a communication link between contradictive subgroups. In order to close the gap, you need to conduct a purposeful search for a common meaning without creating intra-group opposition.

One way to do this is to form a Group Acceptance Pact (GAP). The GAP is an agreement, preferably in writing, to establish a forum where group learning and understanding are sought, where judgment is suspended, and agreement is not necessary. Acceptance is a critical factor in getting low performers to broaden their expectations enough to feel secure in a group. Underachievers are more likely to acknowledge the views of others if they are first accepted "as is" and not pressured to change as a condition of belonging.

The Group Acceptance Pact is simple to design. The following guidelines provide an opportunity for underachievers to practice self-responsibility in the safety of a mutually supportive group environment:

Keep focused
- Stick to the agenda.
- Do not bring up unrelated issues.
- Talk about one issue at a time.
- Fully explore each item before moving on.

Speak without blame
- Share only what you know first hand.
- Be truthful about what happened.
- Avoid faultfinding.
- Seek all the facts.

Comment without judgment
- Listen to ideas, thoughts, and recommendations.
- Resist speaking for or against suggestions.
- Avoid using gestures to express your concerns.
- Do not explain one person's thoughts to another.

Set aside attachments
- Avoid aligning yourself in advance of the meeting.
- Be open to all possibilities during the meeting.
- Leave your personal agenda outside the meeting.
- Do not lobby others for support in the meeting.

Search for meaning
- Provide explanations as often as requested.
- Encourage comments, questions, and clarifications.
- Look for the best in whatever is said.
- Ask for examples of how things might work.

Acknowledge others
- Encourage silent members to provide input.
- Pay attention to each person as they speak.
- Observe a pause after each speaker is finished.
- Briefly summarize each speaker's main points.

Participate fully
- Avoid side comments and conversations.
- Do not interrupt the person talking.
- Take frequent breaks to keep everyone fresh.
- Restrict outside telephone calls and messages.

Trust the process
- Do not change the process once it has begun.
- If the process is not working, ask for suggestions.
- Ask others how they feel about what is going on.
- Discuss why you feel the process is not working.

Managers who use the Group Acceptance Pact (GAP) discover that it greatly enhances the acceptance and implementation of team building, joint decision-making, group problem solving, and collaborative conflict resolution. The payoff comes from those participants who, by practicing self-discovery, are no longer dependent upon management to solve their problem. As a result they become self-directed problem solvers who can think for themselves.

Now that you have armed them with a new set of skills, it is time for the underachievers to take on more responsibility. A more equitable distribution of accountability will lead to higher levels of performance. Shifting the responsibility will also bring more balance to the team and strengthen their interpersonal relationships.

Chapter 6 — Learning

Even Doers sometimes lack the motivation to consistency perform at higher levels. Under adverse or antagonistic conditions, they may need reminding that the purpose of their job is to continuously upgrade what goes out the door—be it products or services.

There are times, however, when the desire to improve is just not there. What are you going to do when that happens? You could wait until the spirit moves them again or you could show those within your sphere of influence how to become self-motivated learners.

Assuming you take the proactive approach, the first question you have to ask is: Do they recognize the need to improve? If the answer is no, then that is where you start.

If the answer is yes, then the next question is: Are they motivated to learn new skills? If that answer is yes, then offer to provide coaching and training.

Conversely, if the answer is no, then your objective is clear: Get them ready to learn by making them aware of what they do not know and why it is important to acquire additional knowledge.

Learning can be a motivating experience provided the learners are fully aware of their shortcomings before the training begins. They will also be energized by the prospect of applying their newly acquired skills to the job.

Creating A Learning Environment

When a company is losing ground to a competitor, management should seek to discover why their products or services are less attractive to customers. Managers should also be concerned about their own competence, asking themselves such questions as:

1) How long is what I know going to be good enough?

2) What will I need to learn in the next 6 - 12 months?

Self-examination is healthy. It is the primary means by which a person can be motivated to learn something new.

Typically, non-performers have little interest in learning without some external stimulation. Understanding how learning takes place progressively in four stages could be very useful to anyone in a leadership position. Armed with this knowledge you can put on your motivator hat and light a fire under some of your least productive followers.

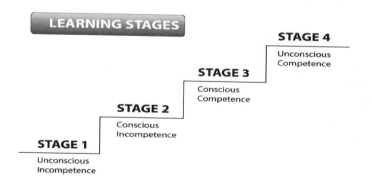

Figure 6 — Learning Stages

Stage 1 - Unconscious Incompetence

They are unaware of the possibility that they may be making costly mistakes or turning out poor quality work. Their unacceptable performance is obvious to others, but not to them. The potential for incompetency is high because they are not motivated to learn new skills.

Stage 2 - Conscious Incompetence

Suddenly they become aware that their performance is having a negative effect on production. They are acutely, perhaps even painfully, mindful of their shortcomings. Now is a good time to improve their skills because their motivation to learn is high and they are ready.

Stage 3 - Conscious Competence

They are in a comfort zone pleased with their newfound knowledge. They have overcome adversity and improved their performance. They proudly seek opportunities to demonstrate their recently acquired skills. Their motivation to learn has been satisfied.

Stage 4 - Unconscious Competence

They perform their job with little thought being given to preparing for new challenges. Unaware of their potential shortcomings, they are only a short step away from losing their competitive edge. Satisfied with the status quo, they have no motivation to learn.

Joe's Dilemma

Joe was a machine operator in a high-tech manufacturing company. His story is a good example of how the learning process applies in a competitive enterprise.

As a loyal employee, Joe had been running the cutting machine for years with no complaints. Things began to change when the production quota was raised and Joe's rejection rates started to climb. Whenever one of the quality checkers tried to tell him about the high number of defects, Joe got upset, saying, "This is my machine and no one tells me how to run it." He continued working in the same old inefficient way. (Stage 1)

Joe was unaware of his poor performance, yet his incompetence was obvious to everyone else. He would not accept that there was a problem and therefore had no motivation to learn.

Joe's situation changed abruptly one morning when he was told to shut down his old machine and help install a new one. The new machine incorporated the latest computer-assisted technology. Joe panicked because he had no idea how to operate this fancy new monster. (Stage 2)

Suddenly, Joe understood the need to improve his skills. So, like it or not, Joe was motivated to learn because his job was in jeopardy.

After an intensive three weeks of classroom training and on-the-job practice, Joe was able to run the machine at medium speed. He kept up with the workflow and performed almost error free. By applying his newfound knowledge, he was able to cut mostly perfect pieces and meet the current production schedules.

His familiarity with the new machine placed him in a comfortable state of mind and he felt great knowing he was good at his job. (Stage 3)

After a few weeks, Joe began to relax and enjoy his success. Everything was under control. The job had become routine again. Joe's performance was good enough as far as he was concerned. Operating the new machine with confidence, Joe was not looking for ways to improve. (Stage 4)

When the other machine operators had completed their training and practice period, the production pace for was accelerated to the maximum. Joe had settled into a nice, comfortable routine, just like his situation before. As the performance demand increased, it was not long before the quality of his work began to slide. Joe had become incompetent again, but he was not aware of it. He was back where he started. (Stage 1)

The Key To Learning

Put yourself in this situation and think about how you would work with Joe if you were his supervisor. The first thing you would want to determine is whether he is aware that his performance has fallen off again. If not, then your job is to bring it to his attention by making him conscious of his incompetence. If he is aware, then your objective is to motivate him to set his sights higher and support him when he does. Because this is an awkward situation, Joe is eager to learn so he can return to his former level of comfort and confidence.

By accepting the challenge to discover what it is he does not know Joe has just become a Doer. Doers have something special working in their favor: the innate human motivation to do a good job that triggers a willingness to acknowledge their own incompetence. Doers are also willing to put up with a certain amount of discomfort during the learning process in order to experience the end result—recognition of a job well done.

Motivating Large Groups

The best way to address the challenge of motivating large groups is to provide a real-life illustration. The company in this story was doing very well. Motivation was not a problem, at least not until the Board of Directors agreed to merge with a major competitor. On paper, this relationship looked like a dream. In reality, though, it turned into a nightmare.

The dealmakers had some concerns about the merging of two disparate cultures, but they were confident that the differences could be worked out. It was not long before interpersonal conflicts began popping up everywhere. Turnover, which had never been a concern for either company, started to rise—the Doers were leaving. Grievances and complaints flooded into the human resource department. Something had to be done.

An organization-wide training needs assessment revealed specific issues in three areas: conflict management, performance measurement, and interpersonal communications. Ninety percent of the people responding checked those three boxes.

A targeted training program was immediately put together and the call for sign-ups went out. Anticipating a large turnout, the organizers were dumbfounded when only a handful of people signed up.

When the survey results were reanalyzed, it was discovered that the respondents had not listed their own needs, but rather the needs of their counterparts, which explains why so few signed up for training.

The evidence was clear: managers from both companies were unaware that they were communicating poorly, creating conflict, and making life difficult for each other.

The training program was rescheduled and the classes were filled up immediately because the managers from both companies were now motivated to learn together.

Once the former competitors emerged from the training program, they were able to focus less on themselves and more on serving customers in their newly expanded market. After all, that is why they merged.

Learning Is About Getting Better

Each time Doers accept that they do not know something and want to learn what it is, they are signaling their willingness to examine old habits, think in new ways, and acquire additional skills. In this learning mode the needs and interests of the leaders and followers are purposefully called into question, opened up for examination, and carefully measured to determine whether anything is out of alignment.

Once Doers identify the discrepancy and put it back in proper working order, they come away feeling a sense of accomplishment. Confident that they can fix anything, they look forward to doing their job better. The next move can be thought of as the "best practices" stage—a time to show off new skills and set new records. This is a great place to be, which is why Doers enjoy working there.

You may be working for one of those companies that spent hundreds of thousands of dollars, and several years certifying all the managers in the use of a hot selling leadership program, only to have it all scrapped when the CEO departs for greener pastures or finds another quick-fix program that looks better.

Sadly, an enormous amount of time, talent, and treasure are being wasted on one-size-fits-all training programs that focus on personality rather than on purpose. Regardless of how management is defined or what the role of a leader might be, the achievement of purpose should be the ultimate objective. The theory you apply, in my view, is less significant than your ability to get people moving in the right direction.

So, what does this mean to you? For starters, if you want to overcome the dysfunction in your workplace, you may have to alter the way you think, beginning with the assumption that leadership is positional and therefore found mostly at the highest levels.

Another defective assertion you may have to let go of is that to lead you must be visible up front. Not so—might have been true at one time, but not anymore. In fact, sometimes it is better to lead from behind so you can see if everyone is headed in the right direction.

We tend to assume a leader is someone who makes things happen. Leaders also stop things from happening—which is the basis for most performance and productivity problems. In today's customer-focused marketplace, initiating corrections, making adjustments, authorizing refunds are all leadership activities.

To succeed in a competitive global marketplace, organizations need responsible leaders at all levels that can act on the company's behalf at any time, day or night.

History-Future Model

Leadership works best when it is informal and natural. Leadership skills can be acquired on-the-job with practice. Doers come by them naturally, so all they need is the opportunity to apply them. Besides, there is seldom enough time to select and formally train leaders. Finally, it is time we focused less on the personality of a leader and more on the process of leadership.

People do not have to undergo a formal training program in order to learn these functions. Just ensure they are clear on the organization's purpose before they assume either role. The beauty of the History-Future Model shown in Figure 7 is that once the issues have been identified and the purpose is known, the manager and leader functions can be performed by just about anyone in the position to take action.

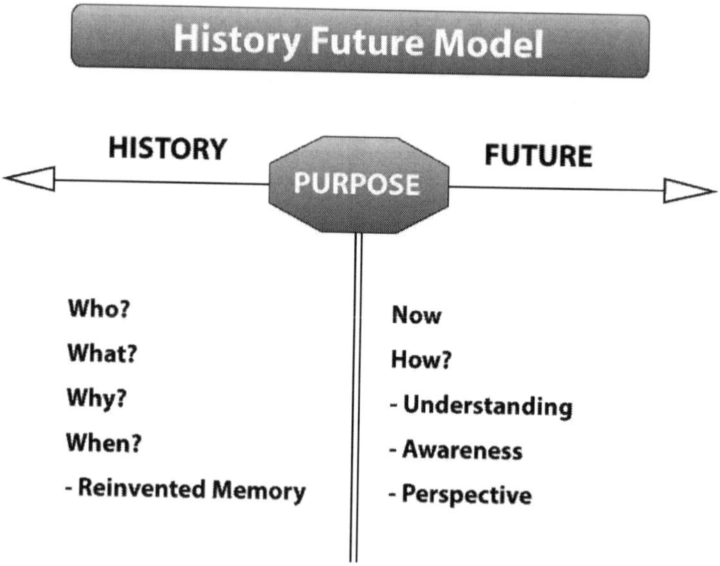

History Future Model

HISTORY		FUTURE

PURPOSE

Who?	Now
What?	How?
Why?	- Understanding
When?	- Awareness
- Reinvented Memory	- Perspective

Figure 7 — History Future Model

Sometimes we make too big a deal about management and leadership development. It has gotten far more complex and time consuming than necessary (not to mention expensive!) So, if you are looking for an easier way to get the job done, the History-Future Model should serve your purpose well.

The History-Future Model is designed for use on the job rather than in a formal training session. It functions best when the people assigned to resolve the issue(s) are brought together to study the situation. This model can also be used as a one-on-one coaching tool.

Start with a quick assessment. A simple show of hands will do. Ask your team to think about the issue or situation at hand that is on the table and indicate if they are "thinking back" or "thinking ahead?" Then ask them to take a position on the side of the room that reflects their current mode of thinking. For example, seat those thinking ahead on the right and ask them to listen as those on the left reflect on the issue(s)

This is a process that may take some time before it becomes automatic and feels normal. It works best if you let it unfold in the most natural way possible. It also helps if the players are familiar with the Group Acceptance Pact set forth in Chapter 5. Determine before you start, how much time you wish to spend on each side of the model. Encourage participants to change sides or take a new position if their focus changes. Ask people to withhold their comments and contributions unless they are sitting with the side that is currently focusing on the issue.

Using the key words shown in the *Manage* column, form a list of questions relevant to the situation. Keep the questions short and simple, like these:

Situation One: Team Performance

- Who are we?
- Why are we here?
- What is our problem?
- When does this happen?

Situation Two: Customer Service

- Who filed the complaint?
- Why are they upset?

- What do they want?
- When do they need it?

Once the focus questions are compiled, the data collection and confirmation can begin. It will not take long before the group's memory of the past is reinvented. At this point, armed with a common pool of knowledge, it is time to shift focus to the *Lead* side of the model. This is also a good place to break and let the players realign themselves for the next round.

Typically, there are a lot more opinions on *what went wrong* than there are about what needs to be done differently. The past is known and therefore much easier to recount. The future is another story—one that has not yet happened and is therefore difficult to talk about in specific terms. For those reasons, you may need to take a more active role in this half of the process.

Working the *Lead* side also starts with the formation of a set of questions. Only, this time each question is prefaced by *Now*, followed by *How*? and is keyed off by the questions on the History list. For example, take the questions from the sample sets above:

Set One: Team Performance

- Now that we know who we are, how often should we get together?
- Now that we know why we are here, how do we proceed?
- Now that we have identified the problem, how do we solve it?
- Now that we know when it happened, how do we prevent it from happening again?

Set Two: Customer Service

- Now that we know who filed the complaint, how do we connect with them?
- Now that we know why they are upset, how do we fix the problem?
- Now that we know what they want, how do we provide it?
- Now that we know when they need it, how do we get it there in time?

Like many new processes, this one takes some getting used to—especially the awkward use of *Now* and *How*. I am not sure why the now-how combination works, but it does help people to stay focused.

The objective of this part of the exercise is to have the entire group gain a better understanding of the problem, a complete awareness of all aspects of the cause, and a sharper perspective on how it should be solved. This can be achieved quickly and is far more practical than working your way through a meeting agenda.

As a rule of thumb, a functional organization, team, or individual should spend between sixty and seventy percent of their energy thinking ahead. Spending too much time on issues from the past is potentially time wasting. You cannot change what has already passed, but you can influence how you respond next time.

Here is an example of how this model was applied to reverse the fortunes of an international manufacturing firm. The company in this case preferred to locate their fabrication plants in rural areas, near small communities known to have a large labor force with a strong work ethic. This strategy had served them well, until recently. During the construction phase of their newest plant, the entire workforce of 500+ employees, supervisors, and managers received training in Total Quality Management methods in addition to an extensive course in Statistical Process Control at the local community college.

The start up went well. Equipment was installed properly and practice runs showed great promise. The first orders were cut to specifications and shipped on time without a hitch. For a while things were looking good. Then the customer complaint hot line started to ring. The majority of complaints fell into two categories: incorrect sizing and shorted orders.

At first, complaints trickled in, but they soon reached a steady flow. Try as they might, the source of the two basic complaints could not be pinpointed. Management called meetings and pushed quality control so hard the workforce got uptight and threatened to form a union. The situation started to get out of hand.

The company president brought in a consultant to look at the new plant operation to see what changes were needed. The consultant was confident that answers would be found by talking with the workers on the production line, so he arranged to visit the night shift.

The shift supervisor scheduled meetings with each of the production crews. Using the two models described above, each group worked its way through the process until the sizing problem was isolated and a resolution found. It turns out that two questions *When does this happen?* and *Who is involved?* provided the key to the solution. It happened on runs with oddly shaped pieces and it involved the machine cutting operators.

Eventually, the sizing problem was traced to the local school board's decision to drop woodworking and metal shop from the high school curriculum several years back. Apparently these classes were the primary source for instruction in the use of a tape measure. Without that basic knowledge the cutters could not tell the difference between 1/16th and 5/8ths of an inch on a tape measure.

To their credit, the machine operators would seek out someone with tape-reading skills to check the first piece of each run. But, if the machines got out of alignment after that, there were no measurements taken before the order was packed for shipping.

The answer to the now, how question led the company to the state office of education where it received a grant to train the plant's entire workforce in basic arithmetic and calculation models.

The shortage problem was harder to find. The answer to *Where does it happen?* took us to the quality checkpoint at the end of the tempering process where the fabricated pieces left the furnace. From there the pieces were picked up by a robot arm and set on a conveyor belt to cool on the way to the final quality check.

When does it happen? pointed us to the checkpoint operator who lifted each piece off the belt and laid it down on a metal frame with electronic sensors around the edges. If the piece did not fit, a loud buzzer would sound indicating rejection. A bell ringing softly meant the piece met specifications and was ready to be wrapped for shipment to the customer. Now we knew the answer to *Why does it happen?* but we still did not know how to fix the problem.

The consultant wandered from line to line waiting to hear a buzzer so he could see for himself *What was causing the deviation?* Sure enough, a buzzer went off nearby and he quickly headed toward the sound.

The checkpoint operator saw him coming and nodded hello as he repeatedly tossed several rejected pieces in the nearby trash bin. The consultant stood beside him to see what he would do next; he did nothing but wait.

The buzzer sounded sporadically for the next twenty minutes. As the two talked between buzzes, the operator seemed very pleased with himself.

Finally, the consultant asked the operator if he was concerned about the high rate of rejection. "Nope," he said, cheerfully. "They know what they are doing. I just pass them when they fit and trash them when they don't." His faced dropped when he was asked *how* "they" would know if he did not tell them.

Later that night, all the checkpoint operators got together with the machine operators to answer the question *Now, that the checker's found a reject, how should he communicate it?*

Confident that they had resolved the shortage problem, the consultant left the crews to their tasks and returned to his hotel for some sleep.

During the next few months, the consultant made several visits to the plant and was encouraged to find the process improvement models being applied throughout the facility.

Production records were being set regularly. Overall, the plant manager had every reason to be pleased with the results; the changes meant his plant would be making a profit well ahead of projections.

Chapter 7 — Accountability

Managers meet regularly to discuss problems, assess progress, and develop strategies. Why is it, then, that the Doers are not afforded this same opportunity? It would seem that getting the high achievers together in the same manner would be just as important. After all, they are in the best position to determine what works and what does not. If given the opportunity, they could also explain why things are not working as planned and what to do about it.

The most frequently offered rationale for not allowing achievers to meet without management supervision is that it would turn in to a gripe session or a waste of time. What management does not realize is that Doers get together anyway at a place of their own called Dirty Ernie's.

Dirty Ernie's is an after hours hangout where Doers feel free to say what is on their minds without the risk of being challenged or corrected by those higher up the chain of command. During working hours Doers are likely to hold a Dirty Ernie's session in the break room, copy center, or cafeteria; anywhere they can talk freely without fear of being overheard.

Surfacing Sensitive Issues

The term Dirty Ernie's can also signal the need for an off-the-record, don't-tell-anyone, you-didn't-hear-it-from-me opportunity to share opinions, test reactions, or generate peer support. Dirty Ernie's sessions are frequently held in the hallway just before and just after a meeting with management.

When Doers are fearful of bringing up troublesome issues in front of their leaders, they gather privately to assess their situation and discuss how best to fix the problem.

Imagine being a fly on the wall at the following real-life Dirty Ernie's session:

A large manufacturer had invested $85 million in the construction of a state of the art fabrication plant that employed the latest in robotics technology. For the most part the installation and testing had gone smoothly. Quality checks showed that production standards were being met or exceeded on every line, but one. Rejections were still running very high on the tempering line. A string of experts had been brought in to identify the cause of the defects, but the source of the problem had eluded them all.

After yet another quality expert had left empty handed or empty headed as the crowd at Dirty Ernie's would claim, a group of check-point operators were overheard teasing each other about having to buy the beers because their crew had lost the "pulling contest." Apparently, two of the supervisors on the swing shift were making friendly bets as to which crew could pack more pieces. It turns out that in order to build up the numbers one of the overzealous supervisors would sometimes slip in pieces that should have otherwise be reworked or discarded.

Later, after the official tally had determined a winner and all the supervisors were gone, the crews would pull the substandard pieces and toss them in the reject pile. The two crews were also running bets themselves as to which supervisor would order them to pack the most rejects.

Rather than alert quality control to the game their supervisors were playing, the crews had instead created a game of their own. Sadly, the company ended up the loser because both sides of the leader-follower equation would rather play games with each other than fix the problem.

Pooling Knowledge

The best way to preempt a situation like the one above is to encourage the Doers to share their concerns openly rather than go to Dirty Ernie's. At first, there will be a period of hesitation and confusion as they look for ways to communicate with directly. To demonstrate how pooling their knowledge in promotes rapid learning and builds trust, bring them together for the following exercise.

Using a dark marking pen place a large **X** on one side of a white coffee mug or plain paper cup and place it in the center of the table where all can see it. Ask for a show of hands of those who can see the **X**.

Point out to those who did not raise their hand that if the **X** represented a vital piece of information, they would have missed it. This simple exercise demonstrates the usefulness of gathering all points of view.

Pooling knowledge becomes especially critical in situations where no one person has the full and complete picture. It also demonstrates the futility of arguing over whether or not there is an **X** on the cup when that is not the problem. Additionally, it points out the need to explore the deeper meaning of a situation whenever the people involved do not agree on what they see.

Anytime there is a dispute, like the **X**-on-the-cup exercise, it should serve as a warning signal that some critical piece of information is missing. It should also trigger the same question in everyone's mind: How might the missing information impact what I do?

In the above exercise the solution to knowledge pooling is simple—just rotate the cup so that those whose views were previously blocked can now see the **X**.

Unfortunately, it is not that simple when these same people are scattered around the organization or in various locations throughout the country and typically do not communicate collectively. There is not likely to be a place where Doers can go to compare their viewpoints and come up with a unifying vision. One way to do this is to create a portable version of the **X**-on-the-cup exercise.

INCLUSIONARY THINKING

The processing of information tends to be exclusionary, that is, hoarded by people who think it gives them power. This method may have worked in the days when decisions were made at the top by a select few. However, in today's workplace everyone needs to have access to all pertinent information.

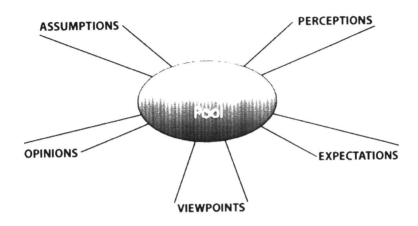

ASSUMPTIONS   PERCEPTIONS

OPINIONS   EXPECTATIONS

VIEWPOINTS

Figure 8 — Inclusionary Thinking

Rather than trickle down from the top as it once did, information instead streams in through a variety of portals. The value of one tiny bit of information cannot be assessed until it has been pooled with other pieces and examined openly. Leaders and followers need to share their perspectives and not go off separately to make decisions.

The key to pooling information and then moving it to the point where it can do the most good is to gather the right people and pose the right questions. Selecting the right people can sometimes be a problem if you are not sure who needs to participate. As a general rule: if in doubt, leave no one out.

As for posing the right questions that can be more challenging. Here is a list of sample questions by category to help get the process started:

Assumptions
- What conclusions have people brought with them?
- What do they actually know?
- What information is missing?
- What are the major agreements and differences?

Opinions
- What do people think should happen?
- Who has taken a stand and who is open to change?
- Are people proactive, reactive or inactive?
- How were their opinions formed and by whom?

Perceptions
- What do people think has happened?
- What information has gotten through?
- What needs correcting or modifying?
- Who is up to date and who is not?

Expectations
- What are the anticipated outcomes?
- What information sources are people using?
- Which expectations are viewed as positive?
- Which expectations are perceived as negative?

Viewpoints
- What do people see from their position?
- What individual views are represented?
- What facts are true and which are being twisted?
- Whose views are blocked and by what or whom?

As the knowledge pooling process begins to take shape, you will understand how the way you pose the questions and respond to answers will determine whether the Doers turn to you when they are frustrated and confused, or go to Dirty Ernie's for reliable answers.

Rumor Control

No matter how positive a spin you put on it, people fear change because it generates confusion and raises their level of distrust. Building trust during a period of transition is a tough job. Rumors run rampant. Even when you try to tell people the truth about what is going on, they still rely on the juicy tidbits they pick up at Dirty Ernie's.

When challenged, those who complain the loudest about "being left out of the loop" confess that even if there were more meetings, more memos, or more information sharing, they would still pay attention to whatever gossip was making the rounds.

It is human nature to ruminate and speculate about other people and how the pending change will affect their lives. This explains why everyone's strengths, weaknesses, hot buttons, and personal problems quickly become grist for the rumor mill.

Here is an illustration of how harmful rumors can be and why you should work hard to control them. A foreign-born research scientist who had just accepted a position in a testing laboratory resigned after only a week because he heard a rumor that his predecessor had been "canned" because of his "funny" accent.

His coworkers jokingly told him that if he did not watch out he would be "canned" too. Even though he spoke English very well, he did not understand the meaning of the term "canned."

When it was explained to him, he chose to resign rather than suffer the humiliation of being fired. He was one of a string of highly skilled, foreign-born scientists who had quit the lab because of rumors that something bad would happen to them because they spoke with an accent.

The rumormongers took great delight in spreading gossip even when they had proof that people suffered as a result. Somehow it gave them a sense of power.

It is true: everyone loves a juicy piece of news. Even if you do not want to believe it, you still want to hear it. The rumor mill usually carries harmless or amusing commentary. Unfortunately, some carriers get a kick out of passing on unfounded rumors or false stories just to get attention. They do not seem to realize that their mean-spirited game playing can harm innocent people.

When this happens, reputations are damaged, credibility is lost, and morale suffers. Perhaps the rumors where you work are not that rough on people. Just in case things do get out of hand, here are a few suggestions you will find useful the next time the rumor mill starts grinding out false information:

Do not wait until you have all the details—just get the truth, as you understand it, out there quickly.

Unless you are bound by some legal restriction, when you get wind of a rumor, share everything you know about the facts of the matter. If some of what you say turns out to be inaccurate, then retell it the right way as soon as you get a chance. You may have to do this several times before a rumor dies.

Pick out Doers who are trustworthy and talk to them collectively. Tell them you want to know what they are hearing. Ask them not to embellish on what they tell you. Let them know that if you find out they have twisted the story even a little bit, you will not rely on them again.

Keep your attitude, comments, and feelings to yourself. Report only the facts that you know first hand.

Listen to individual opinions thoughtfully without comment. This may sound harsh, but, people do not care what you think, nor do they want to hear your opinion. They just want to know what you know, not what you think or feel.

Regardless of how well you communicate; inaccurate information will still work its way throughout the organization. Misinformation can be hurtful to sensitive people, detrimental to the spirit of teamwork, and waste time, energy, and precious resources.

Doers take in information in three ways: they see it, hear it, or feel it. The majority will believe it when they can see it. Even those who use touch and hearing will form a mental image of what they hear or feel before they act. For these reasons, it is important to minimize the negative effect of gossip by putting your vision out there so the Doers can "see" what you mean.

Whoever said, "A picture is worth a thousand words," understood this process very well. Once you have gained their confidence, provide a regular place and time for Doers to get together to discuss their differences and examine their expectations in a supportive environment.

In addition to setting up a regular place and time, you will also need to provide them with a set of meeting guidelines similar to the Group Acceptance Pact (GAP) outlined in Chapter 5. Dirty Ernie's is an open forum where the louder one shouts the more attention one gets.

That type of behavior will not be helpful, which is why they need to follow meeting guidelines. Once they get used to the process they will establish their own format. Meanwhile, providing a set of suggested behaviors shows that you are serious about wanting to make this work for them.

Setting aside time for Doers to interact in a structured assembly greatly enhances the acceptance and implementation of team building, joint decision-making, group problem solving, and conflict resolution throughout the organization.

The payoff comes from those formerly disgruntled Doers who no longer feel the need to take their issues to Dirty Ernie's. They become self-directed information collectors who share critical issues freely with each other and more importantly with you.

Holding Underachievers Accountable

I was once called in to a construction company that was having difficulty finding and keeping a skilled labor pool. In addition to losing good people, they had also lost several costly lawsuits filed by former employees who had been unfairly dismissed. Something had to be done.

After introducing myself at the management meeting, I told the assembly that I was there to learn more about their personnel problems. At first, several people denied having any problems and saw no need for my being there. A quiet voice from the back of the room suggested I was talking to the wrong people. A second person standing along the wall pointed to the Human Resource Director and shouted, "Ask him." Suddenly, an angry attendee jumped up and said he would tell me exactly what was causing all the problems.

"Just the other day," he began, "I sent two new hires out to dig a trench." He went on to explain that he had instructed them to only use shovels. In other words, they were supposed to dig the trench by hand. "How hard can that be?" he chided.

It turned out that when these two guys got to the job site, they realized it would take them all day to do the job by hand with shovels, so they decided to use a mechanical backhoe to get the job done more quickly.

Unfortunately, the backhoe ripped into an underground telephone cable. The damage was extensive and so were the repair costs.

As the angry spokesperson finished recounting his story, he triumphantly announced that he had fired both those "idiots" for not following directions. Rousing applause and loud shouts conveyed approval.

Probing deeper, I asked the still-fuming manager if he had known about the telephone cable before assigning the task. "Sure," he said, "That is why I told them to use hand tools. I assumed they would uncover the cable and dig around it." I suggested that the incident could have been avoided, had he shared this critical information with the workers, especially since they were new hires. "That is none of their business!" he bellowed. "People who can't follow simple directions have no business being hired."

For the rest of the meeting I listened to similar stories about damaged equipment, safety violations, poor job performance, and the lack of accountability all of which they blamed on poor hiring practices. It was clear that they held the Human Resource Director accountable for all their problems with the workforce.

Effective leaders, unlike those in this story, must accept accountability for their actions, or lack thereof, and for those of their followers. Before people will follow a leader, they must first understand and accept what is expected of them. They also need to know the best way to interact with others on their team.

Doers know what they are being held accountable for and are able to determine for themselves how best to follow their leader. Underachievers seldom understand their own actions; so do not expect them to give much constructive thought to what their leader has in mind.

So, you might ask, why waste time on non-productive employees? Why not leave them alone and concentrate solely on the high performers? That is a workable strategy as long as everyone's job remains the same and the organization never changes. Dysfunction is most easily exposed when an organization undergoes change. Here is why that happens.

Ineffective managers, like those in the cable story above, view change as an opportunity to get rid of the "dead wood." Research into the after effects of organization-wide changes, such as an expansion or a downsizing, point to a chilling conclusion: dead wood floats. When low performers hear about an upcoming change, they immediately focus on keeping their job not on getting better at doing it.

Doers have external networks that keep them in touch with external job openings. They also have the confidence to look beyond their current employer. As the competition gets wind of their availability, the best people are often hired away just at the time when they are most needed. Underachievers lack the confidence to look elsewhere, so they are not likely to receive an outside job offer.

As the change begins to take shape, a shadow competition unfolds between the Doers and the poor performers. The term shadow is used because management is usually in the dark about what is really happening. There are several behaviors that will tip you off to when and why such a competition is taking place.

Underachievers will stand together in pointing out the faults and failures of their high performing coworkers. One common technique is for two of them to hang around after a meeting, hoping to catch their leader alone. Once they have the leader cornered, they claim that it is hard for them to say something negative about a Doer, but they thought the leader ought to know that some of his or her high achievers are looking for other jobs.

They finish with a personal declaration of loyalty and then offer to take on more work if necessary. They hope to gain favor by casting doubt on their high performing coworkers. Meanwhile the Doers, tired of being asked to pick up the slack, are sending out their resumes, looking for better opportunities elsewhere.

Because low performers have more at stake in staying put, they are more likely to "fight" for their jobs. Under-performers can cover up their fears and hold their feelings in check when things are going their way. But those fears are always waiting to crop up when they are antagonized by potential changes in the status quo.

When pushed to respond to the ambiguity and inconsistency typically associated with change, under achievers become fearful of being held accountable because their shortfalls may be exposed. They must first trust that they will be treated fairly if they do make mistakes and given the opportunity to fix what is broken. It is management's responsibility to create a workplace where Doers flourish and underachievers can practice getting better.

Chapter 8 — Initiative

When supervisors respond to surveys asking them to name which job duties they most often avoid or postpone, performance management tops the list. In follow-up interviews they further acknowledge having neither the confidence nor the competence to take on this unpopular task, choosing instead to transfer, ignore, or demote those who show little initiative in the hope they will get the message and seek employment elsewhere.

So, you might ask, what is wrong with writing off those with low initiative and concentrating solely on the Doers?

Unfortunately, many leaders are doing just that. Sadly, they soon find that it does not work because the Doers resent having to carry the workload and start looking elsewhere for equity.

If you want the Doers to stick around, you must find a way to raise the level of initiative of those under-performers within your sphere of influence.

A word of caution: just bringing up the subject of initiative is going to generate a wide range of reactions. Doers might interpret what you are proposing as a license to do their own thing independent of your direction. Those who you wish would show more initiative will want to discuss all options with you before they act on any.

You will need to consider carefully what you mean when you tell an under-performer to "show more initiative." It may sound like a positive request, but without a clear understanding of what you both think it means, showing more initiative may not always be the best response.

Initiative Levels

The first thing to consider is how much initiative do you want your potential Doers to have. Once you have conveyed the options, they will be in a better position to select a level that is most comfortable for you both. It is best to start a potential Doer at level 1, 2, or 3. Later, you can raise or lower the level depending upon how well he or she performs. You can also make adjustments as conditions and circumstances change.

Most likely the Doers will want to operate at level 4, 5, or 6. Therefore, it is up to you to create the conditions where that can happen. In other words, build the level of trust to the point where the Doers do not have to worry about how far they can go on their own before you rein them in when you get nervous.

Level 1: Wait for direction - Expecting potential Doers to jump right out there and do what they think is best is not always a good strategy when conditions are uncertain. In that case, it is probably better to have them wait for updated or accurate information before taking action.

Take for instance the sales staff of a national clothing manufacturer who was using outdated pricing and inventory lists to take orders and schedule deliveries. After profits plummeted and several of the firm's top salespeople quit, management upgraded the information system and provided each salesperson with online connection capability using a laptop computer.

Departments would post cutting and production schedules and current quantity discount prices twice daily in each region or upon specific request whenever a salesperson needed authorization to close a special order. It was not long before the sales force broke all existing performance records.

Level 2: Ask for direction - There are times when potential Doers should ask for direction, especially when events do not unfold as previously planned. Expecting them to just sit around waiting for direction when faced with a situation that needs immediate attention is not a good strategy.

Picture a busy doctor telling his receptionist to cancel all appointments and hold all calls because an important visitor is expected shortly. The visitor arrived soon after and was told by the receptionist that the doctor had just directed her to cancel all appointments and hold all calls. The visitor assumed an emergency had come up so he wrote a note on his business card and left it with the secretary.

Soon after, the doctor came out to ask if the visitor had arrived yet and was handed the note. He was dumbfounded to learn that the important visitor had come and gone without a word from the receptionist. Had she asked the doctor for a name or details in order to identify the visitor, this story would have ended happily.

Level 3: Suggest a direction - Those potential Doers who deal with the product or provide the service know better than anyone else why something is not working the way it should and what to do about it. Their ideas will not be forthcoming, however, unless they are encouraged to share their views and make suggestions.

For example, a home health agency in a large metropolitan area was putting pressure on its nursing staff to see more patients. Under the current system, the nurses would begin their day at the central office where they would be assigned a patient from the list. After each visit, the nurse would then drive back to the office to pick up the next assignment. Operating in this system a nurse could make three to four home visits per day. Not enough to sustain the financial goals set forth by the Board of Directors.

The nurses came up with two great suggestions. First, they were each provided a mobile phone so that they could call in for assignments instead of coming to the office. Second, rather than assign the next patient from the list, the nurse calling in would be assigned the patient nearest to his or her current location. When the numbers were tallied at the end of the trial period, home visits had doubled and transportation costs were cut in half.

Level 4: Act and report immediately - Veteran Doers are in the best position to prevent conditions from getting worse or to improve upon the situation as they see fit. Established Doers should be preauthorized to cope with issues first and then report the results of their actions right away.

Here is a great example. Benny the purchasing clerk had established a reputation for wheeling and dealing with vendors. The new administrator found out recently just how good Benny was when he placed an order for a multipurpose document copier. While shopping around, Benny came upon a great deal on a state-of-the-art machine.

Shipping and installation costs would be waived if the order were placed immediately. Unfortunately, the total cost was more than the amount stated on the purchase order. Rather than wait for another requisition, Benny gave the go ahead. As soon as the deal was struck, Benny nervously tracked down the administrator to obtain his approval. Much to Benny's relief, the administrator was not only pleased with the decision, but also grateful to Benny for taking the initiative.

Level 5: Act and report periodically - Experienced Doers know when a situation has the potential for worsening if action is not taken to resolve the problem on the spot. Such preauthorized actions should be recorded and later reported at regular weekly or monthly meetings.

Jerry, the project team leader, had what he hoped was great news for his colleagues. For months, the team had been spread out around the small campus crammed into cubicles and tiny windowless rooms. Eager to be housed in the same building, Jerry had been given the seemingly impossible task of finding a place large enough to match their space requirements and budget limitations.

Shortly after, a local realtor called to say that a bankrupt firm had just been evicted from a building that sounded perfect. Eager to have a tenant, the landlord agreed to forego three months' rent and the security deposit if they would accept the space as is and move in immediately. Jerry signed the lease, confident that this is just what the team needed. His announcement a week later at the regular meeting was met with a jubilant round of applause.

Level 6: Act until redirected - Self-directed Doers are confident in their ability to negotiate agreements, overcome challenges, and respond to deviations. Doers at this level are secure in the knowledge that they have unconditional support from above.

Here is an example of how a Doer can achieve more than expected when given free rein. Chris was assigned responsibility for creating a world-class conference center at a regional children's hospital. As Director of Training and Development, he knew that the budget was significantly smaller than the challenge he faced.

Rather than compete for additional funding, Chris instead convinced the other departments to combine their training budgets. He arranged internships for Instructional Technology students from the local university to design and install the audiovisual system.

Brand new, state-of-the-art equipment was donated by local businesses that in turn received tax credits. The center was soon hosting top-rated conferences for physicians and medical educators from all over the world as well as providing training programs, workshops, and seminars for the hospital staff.

Performance Coaching

Now that you have a handle on the initiative issue, the next step is to put on your coaching hat and start looking for solutions to what is preventing the low performers from reaching higher.

Performance Management and Process Improvement are easy-to-use feedback tools that expose whatever might be blocking a potential Doer's path to success. Once these factors are opened up for discussion, both the coach and the impacted performer will understand how best to unblock the pathway to greater productivity.

The least threatening way to introduce Performance Management and Process Improvement is to frame a set of questions in the form of a checklist that follows the natural workflow. For example:

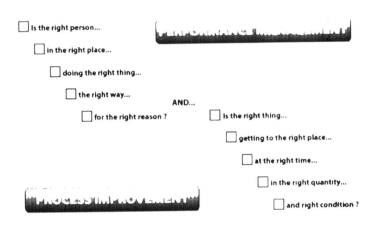

Figure 9 — Process Improvement

Now with the impacted individual at your side, work your way slowly through the checklists until you can both confidently answer yes to every question. This process may take multiple sessions; do not be in a hurry to complete the checklist the first time out.

Here is an example of how a product line supervisor applied Performance Management and Process Improvement to address the productivity of a new employee who came to the job with few expectations other than a steady paycheck.

Shortly after completing the orientation program, Susan was introduced to the other members of her work team who made her feel welcome. It was not long, however, before Susan ran into trouble. She was making a lot of mistakes and falling behind, but she showed no outward signs of concern.

When her supervisor came by one day to see how she was doing, Susan said everything was okay. The next morning, Susan found herself in the supervisor's office. Instead of being upset, her supervisor presented a flowchart of how the output of Susan's job impacted the workflow of others in the department. As she responded to her supervisor's queries, Susan realized the importance of her place in the production flow and why the company depended upon her to do the right thing, the right way, for the right reason.

Susan's supervisor went on to explain why she should be thinking about the highest and best use of her time and talent so as not to miss an opportunity to improve the quality of her work. The supervisor made it clear that whenever Susan found it difficult to keep up, she should not be afraid to say so.

Relieved to know she still had a job, Susan asked for additional training and promised to try harder. Her supervisor approved the training with the stipulation that Susan would schedule periodic performance reviews. Susan now understood that she was expected to take responsibility for her own performance.

Susan, like many new hires, believed that all she had to do to ensure her future was to find a good job with a good company that offered good pay and good benefits. After that, it is just a matter of doing what one is told and not taking any risks. Little thought is given to how individual performance relates to collective productivity.

One purpose of Performance Management, then, is to provide underachievers with an awareness of why getting it right is important coupled with an understanding of what they need to do differently in order to have a future with the organization.

At this stage of development, former underachievers are ready to consider the highest and best use of their abilities. Your task now is to develop ways to retain those who reach Doer status. The retention factors listed below will ensure that those who do reach Doer status have reason to stay with your organization and continue their excellent work.

Doers are the backbone of the workforce. They do the right things the right way for the right reasons and provide the initiative for new ideas and the energy that drives productivity. These attributes are highly prized by employers who see attracting a steady flow of Doers as essential to the prosperity of their organization.

Attracting And Retaining Doers

Good people are always hard to find. The best candidates will check out your reputation thoroughly before they even consider showing up for an interview. With that in mind here are seven ways for an organization to establish the reputation it will need to attract and retain Doers.

1) During the interview process communicate the right message, and make sure it is accurate. If you want to attract good people, you cannot just flash dollar signs

before their eyes. You must be able to convey that they will be esteemed for who they are, for their unique skills, and for the value they add to the organization. External motivators like salary and benefits now have a limited shelf life. The enduring attractions to Doers are the opportunity to grow in their profession, to make a meaningful difference, and to achieve something within an organization they could not accomplish on their own.

2) During the first two weeks on the job, make the new hires feel welcome. Reconfirm three points: 1) the reason they were hired, 2) what you expect of them, and 3) how their contributions will be measured. The challenge is to connect new employees as soon as they are hired and not let them swim around in circles struggling to keep their head above water. Doers want to know from the start that what they are doing is in line with their own career objectives as well as appropriate for the company.

3) Assign peer coaches and mentors to guide new employees, rather than criticizing, ignoring or teasing them. What makes new hires feel most welcome during their first few days on the job is how their peers treat them. Being ridiculed or made the brunt of pranks and jokes creates an atmosphere of animosity. Research shows that it is the most competent, functional workers who are the first to flee a hostile environment. Veterans have an important part to play in bringing rookies up to speed and helping them to fit in fast and find job satisfaction quickly.

4) Ensure that someone at the executive level is always available to solve significant problems. This lets Doers know that the chain of command is working and that someone with authority is easy to locate. The designated executive needs to be inside the company, not away at a conference or tied up in a meeting. When senior leaders are accessible, Doers have the satisfaction and the validation of receiving feedback from those they respect. One cannot underestimate how inspiring this is.

5) Expect managers to form teams and act in a team-like fashion. If Doers do not see teamwork modeled from above, there is no inspiration for them to make the necessary compromises to work together cooperatively. Companies without teamwork develop a reputation for dissent, not cooperation. Doers then feel disconnected and vulnerable, especially during times of change, and they can find no collective sense of accomplishment. In addition, it is hard for them to measure their own growth because they feel as if they are operating in a vacuum. An achiever cannot have an accurate sense of accomplishment if he or she is the only one measuring.

6) Insist that supervisors give frequent evaluations, provide honest feedback, and address poor performance and inappropriate behavior in a timely way. Evaluations contribute to the overall morale of the workforce; the immediate feedback clears up confusion, reinforces excellence, and helps reassure people that their growth within the company is on track. Hard work is recognized, which provides Doers with the incentive to reach for even loftier goals.

Addressing poor performance is important because it reassures Doers that the company's status as a place that rewards excellence and discourages substandard work is well deserved.

7) Create an atmosphere where Doers can make complaints, acknowledge criticism, challenge inconsistencies, and communicate negative information upward without risk of retribution. These behaviors establish the organization as a place where open communication is the norm. Doers want assurances that they will, in fact, be supported for trying to rectify problems, not penalized for it, that honesty counts, and that they do not have to suffer the frustration of avoiding the truth. Achievers must trust that their mistakes can be corrected without fear that it will be held against them and hamper their career path. In the end, the only thing that should be measured or remembered is success.

Contrary to popular beliefs about the cold-hearted world of work, business is still about people and how they work together. But workplace relationships take time to develop, and in this day of rapid change and fast turnaround, time is at a premium.

The first thing to suffer is often the rapport between Doers. In this tight employment market a business must foster an environment that promotes harmony, boosts morale, supports creativity, encourages honest communication, and reduces anxiety.

It is easy to see why attracting Doers and then keeping them from leaving is more important than ever. The expenditures involved in recruiting good people and then losing them are high—up to 300% of the first year's salary.

In fact, if the problem is serious it can significantly impact the company's bottom line. A recent Wall Street Journal poll showed that businesses with stable, highly committed Doers enjoy greater profits than those with high turnover.

Chapter 9 — Dysfunction

Workplace dysfunction occurs whenever the Doers lack the confidence and desire to work together toward a common purpose.

Much like a contagious disease, dysfunction spreads from person to person and from unit to unit. If the condition is left undiagnosed, an entire organization can become dysfunctional and not know it is "sick."

Every disease has a beginning, a place or a point where it started. The same is true for dysfunction; it does not happen overnight.

A typical work unit moves through four stages on its way to becoming dysfunctional. Some may reach Stages I and II and remain there during a period of transition, while others may continue moving, unchecked, toward Stages III and IV.

It is common in this day of rapid change, data processing, and information overload for a company to hover between Stages I and II and still remain functional.

Signs of more harmful dysfunction begin to appear when the organization settles into Stage III. If Stage IV is reached, the evidence is not easy to spot and therefore more difficult to overcome.

By understanding the various conditions that define each stage, you may be able to intervene and bring about a productive change before the dysfunction reaches the higher stages and sets in permanently.

Stages Of Dysfunction

Stage 1 - Ambiguities are not questioned.

A new directive can be interpreted more than one way. Two supervisors interpret the intention differently and give conflicting instructions to their teams. The impacted employees do not ask for clarification, even though doing so would relieve their anxiety. Instead, they wait for the ambiguities to be clarified by someone in authority.

Stage 2 - Inconsistencies are ignored.

Employees who carpool consistently arrive late; nothing is said. Others, who travel independently, are reprimanded for not being on time. When the disciplined employees finally complain to management, they are told that the issue is being looked into. They are told to mind their own business and the situation continues, unchanged.

Stage 3 - Ambiguities and inconsistencies are discussable.

No one is willing to recognize there are serious problems which employees are reluctant to discuss openly. Silence during meetings not only infers that problems do not exist; it also implies that nothing be said regarding any actions management might take to address problems.

Stage 4 - Undiscussability is undiscussable.

In response to a drastic drop in productivity, a morale survey is conducted. The findings show that both employee confidence and job satisfaction are low. Three department heads and the human resources manager are suddenly fired. It is business as usual at the next general management meeting. No one mentions the purge.

STAGE 1 Ambiguity is not Questioned

STAGE 2 Inconsistancies are Ignored

STAGE 3 Ambiguities and Inconsistencies are Undiscussable

STAGE 4 Undiscussability is Undiscussable

Figure 10 — Stages of Dysfunction

By now you may be ready to assess the level of dysfunction that currently exists in your area of responsibility. Armed with this knowledge, you will be in a better position to develop a set of practical strategies that have a two-pronged purpose:

1. To reinforce functional behaviors.
2. To discontinue dysfunctional practices.

Overcoming dysfunction and restoring functionality is not all doom and gloom. There will be some rough times, but for the most part, you will enjoy seeing your coworkers recognize their dysfunction and openly acknowledge the need to change their behaviors.

Keep this guiding principle in mind as you work toward functionality in your sphere of influence: Dysfunctional coworkers are not bad people and most likely are unaware that their behavior is impeding team performance.

Dysfunctional Behaviors Checklist

The following list describes behavioral traits that are commonly observed in a dysfunctional workplace. Are any of the behaviors on this list common in your organization? Check them off and use the results to assess the level of dysfunction.

As you set about to restore functionality, use the specific items you have checked to develop an action plan. If you really feel brave, give a copy of the Dysfunctional Behaviors Checklist to your coworkers to complete. Then bring them together to share the results. The comparison would make an interesting and worthwhile discussion topic for your next team meeting.

1. Communication is indirect.

People do not talk to each other face-to-face. Instead, they find an alternative method of conveying information, especially if the message is bad news, likely to create hard feelings, or may bring up an uncomfortable issue. This method is frequently used between individuals or groups who have a long-standing feud or just do not get along. A third party may be asked to deliver the message but instructed not to reveal the sender's identity.

2. Conflicts are not stated openly.

Differences between coworkers remain hidden from the collective view. People keep track of what upsets others and make certain not to bring up these deeper issues for fear of incurring the wrath of the affected party. Personal frustration and misdirected anger stimulate spirited debates centered on non-threatening issues such as where to hold the Christmas party, which supply vendor to use, or who is authorized to park in the reserved spaces.

3. Secrets are used to build alliances.

Individuals with confidential or privileged information disclose it to a chosen few. Sensitive information is passed with this caveat attached: Promise you will not tell anyone. If it gets out that I told you, I am in big trouble. In turn, these confidants are expected to share any private tidbits that come their way. Thus, an alliance is formed of insiders who feel involved and included. Meanwhile, those outside the alliance feel alienated and excluded.

4. Gossip is used to excite and titillate.

Everyone loves a juicy piece of gossip. Even if they do not want to believe it, they still want to hear it. The rumor mill usually carries harmless or amusing commentary. Unfortunately, some folks get a kick out of passing on unfounded or false stories just to get attention. The mean-spirited passing of false accusations and malicious heresy harms innocent people; reputations are damaged, credibility is lost, and employee morale suffers.

5. Corporate memory is lost or forgotten.

Records of verbal agreements cannot be found. Projects get started and then stop suddenly without explanation. Problems that were thought to have been resolved suddenly resurface. Work is often duplicated for no apparent reason while similar tasks are forgotten or ignored. Quick fixes replace carefully thought and previously agreed upon solutions, and past mistakes are repeated. The primary mission is lost in a sea of special programs and pet projects.

6. Requests for policy clarification are ignored.

Those who raise policy questions in an open forum are frequently told "I will get back to you on that," or "Let me run that one by HR," or "Stop by my office later and we can talk about it." If the requesters do stop by, they are provided with justification rather than clarification. Written requests for policy guidance go unanswered. Direct questions about policy implementation are met with hostility, but no answer.

7. The open expression of true feelings is absent.

People feel uncomfortable expressing how they really feel due to fear of being judged or criticized. If people know their feelings will not be respected, they keep them hidden. Even when they strongly oppose the prevailing viewpoint, they nod and give their approval. A show of feelings is avoided for fear of getting hurt. Those who do share their feelings out are labeled as too touchy-feely.

8. The search for the cause of a problem is personalized.

The key concern is who was wrong rather than what went wrong. Anyone with information keeps quiet until the search is over. People spend more time covering their tracks than solving problems. The guilty parties are mentioned by name and held up as bad examples. Taking responsibility leads to blame, when things go wrong.

9. People look for direction on how to act and react.

People hesitate to go ahead on their own because they have learned that even when told it is up to you, it is not. Folks decode body language and read between the lines looking for hidden agendas. Trial balloons are floated up the chain of command to test reactions and make sure upstairs is okay with it. Projects are piloted repeatedly to work out all the bugs before the final launch. Missed completion dates are blamed on endless red tape.

10. Socialization between coworkers is lacking.

Folks who work together do not seem to know much about each other. Opportunities for personal interaction after hours are rare and not well attended. People are seldom asked, and rarely volunteer, what is going on in their lives outside the workplace. Misunderstandings, mistrust, and miscommunications are taken for granted. Occasions for celebration, like birthdays, anniversaries, awards, and promotions, come and go with little fanfare.

11. Complex procedures are initiated by memorandum.

Major projects such as computer conversions, systems installations, and office relocations are suddenly jump-started by a vaguely worded email. Practical guidelines are hard to find. Planning session schedules are rarely followed. When asked to provide details, project managers promise to provide the relevant information as it becomes available. That day never comes.

12. Long meeting agendas end up going in circles.

New business is added after the agenda is published. Those who are not satisfied with the previous decision revisit old business. Personal agendas are injected by the use of phrases like: This will only take a minute; I hope no one has a problem with this; There is just one thing that concerns me; I am not sure I agree, totally. Meetings sometimes run so long that people will agree to anything just to get out of there.

13. Inconsistent application of procedures is not challenged.

Chaos and confusion typically follow the introduction of a new procedure. Directives are followed by some but not by others, resulting in two different outcomes. No one points out the inconsistency or seeks clarification. When policies seem unfair or discriminatory, no one says anything. People work outside their job descriptions and expertise without complaining. When procedural changes are introduced at meetings, those most impacted sit quietly without comment.

14. Mundane reviews and reports replace serious issues on the meeting agenda.

In contrast to having important issues to talk about the instructions for completing a survey of photocopy needs are covered in detail. The food service director presents a categorized list of menu changes with the nutritional value of each item. A discussion of the facilities maintenance schedule and equipment replacement projections, tabled at the last session, will continue if time allows.

15. Promises of better times ahead seduce people into a status quo.

An unexpected rash of resignations is shrugged off as a knee-jerk reaction to a temporary down turn. Motivational speeches and morale building sessions increase for no apparent reason. Higher profit and sales forecasts are announced with great fanfare. The long-term growth projections are unrealistic, but most people accept the numbers. Doers pull together, and give 110% although their reasons for doing so are not realistic.

16. Dualistic (us vs. them) thinking creates conflict and sets up sides.

People are forced to take a stand either for or against when opposing viewpoints surface. Alternative options or compromise solutions are seldom explored. The challenge to be right simulates opposing parties. People choose their side carefully because being on the losing end can have negative consequences. Managers voice sarcastic threats to ensure allegiance: "Remember who signs your check," and "My way or the highway," are two examples.

17. Perfectionism creates an atmosphere of intolerance for mistakes.

Micromanagers control every outcome. No matter how hard people work, or how good they get, they are expected to do more. Criticism prevails while praise and recognition are nonexistent. Simple mistakes and innocent oversights are blown out of proportion. Employees are disciplined or demoted for minor infractions. Those who complete assignments ahead of schedule are given more work to do. Enough is never enough.

18. Judgments are made about people and things being "good" or "bad."

People are told: That is a *bad* idea. It is a *good* thing you checked with me first. Promotions are based on how well people "fit." Personality is a critical factor in determining who gets along with whom. Employees who do not fit in are labeled as "bad" and rarely given a second chance. A "good" employee is one who gets along well with coworkers and does not upset the boss. Job performance and quality work does not seem to matter.

19. Isolation keeps management from seeing what is happening.

Employees feel that management is out of touch and has no idea of what is going on. Long-standing personnel problems never get resolved. Complaints and concerns are ignored. Managers are too often out of town, away at a conference, or in a meeting. Electronic messaging and digital technologies buffer management from the world outside. Management has no idea what is important to the people who work for them. Two-way communication between leaders and followers is nonexistent.

20. Management isolation is used as the basis of decision-making by cliques.

Like-minded people assemble in small groups and set their own agenda. Groups compete for scarce resources and purposely withhold information from each other. Those who show initiative are thought to have management's protection. Department heads with connections seem to get whatever equipment and personnel they need. Those outside the loop are still waiting for approval. Participants assume that if management knows, they must not care.

The above checklist is offered as an introduction to the type of dysfunction that may be present within your sphere of influence. As you strive to restore functionality, you may discover new or additional behaviors.

If so, add them to your action plan. Dysfunction is not a permanent condition, but it does develop progressively if no action is taken to stem its progress at the lower stages.

Shifting Attention

Much like a house remodeling will expose termites, organization-wide undertakings such as quality improvement, team building, reinventing, or downsizing will flush out dysfunction. The problems that arise from the installation of a new software program or a computer upgrade can shift management's attention in a hurry.

For example, a department head had not planned to get involved in office relocation project, but there he was settling the argument over who would get the window office and where to put the new desks and chairs. Whenever there is a lot more going on than expected, it is a sign that dysfunction has been uncovered.

Then there was the time a supervisor tried to adjust the work schedule and found himself in meeting after meeting with upper management and the union rep explaining his intention. Later, when he suggested a cross-training program for the newly hired staff, "all hell broke loose."

Large organizations are good places for dysfunction to hide. To find it, a leader must focus on each work unit separately. In doing so, he or she should be alert for problems that are attributed to individual personalities.

For example, a group of employees may candidly tell their supervisor that they are having problems with Mr. Teflon, and if management got rid of him, things would get better. But when the leader tries to focus on exactly what Mr. Teflon has done to deserve their mistrust, none of their complaints or accusations ring true.

There really was a Mr. Teflon and much like the coating on a frying pan, nothing stuck to him. This nickname was once given to a manager who gave ambiguous directives that almost always needed clarification. If his subordinates got things right, he took the credit. When things went awry, even though they had acted on the information he had given them, he denied ever having given those directions.

He frequently said things off-the-record to one person while sharing a slightly altered version of the same confidential information with another. When the two subordinates got together and compared confidences they discovered Mr. Teflon's duplicity. When they shared their concerns with coworkers they discovered that this was typical of how he turned people against each other.

I was working there on one occasion when this happened and was asked to confront Mr. Teflon during a meeting with his subordinates. When presented with a list of names and specific statements, he acted surprised and denied having said anything.

When his staff, one by one, repeated what he had told them; Mr. Teflon skillfully shifted the blame, declaring, "Well, I may have said it, but you should not have told anyone else. I thought we had agreed to keep that confidential. Even if I did say what you say I said, which I didn't, you had no right to pass it on."

He admonished them for violating his confidence, and abruptly ended the session by declaring that he would no longer trust them. The group realized that despite their honest effort, none of their allegations had stuck. After that experience, they completely lost their trust in him. The sad thing is, they also stopped trusting each other.

A change in senior management is less likely to stir up dysfunction than a change of mid-level supervisor or lead person. It seems that management changes at the higher levels have minimal influence on what happens at the operational level. A change in department heads might go unnoticed, but replacing a shift foreman can have a dramatic impact on production—and, consequently, on organizational priorities.

Today's instantaneous electronic messaging can also facilitate dysfunctional behaviors. As people rely less on face-to-face communications and more on texting and social media, they pay less attention to established policies, standards, and procedures. Speed is often obtained at the expense of accuracy and reliability.

In a dysfunctional workplace, electronic communications in the form of emails and texts messages are highly susceptible to misinterpretation. Underachievers do not bother seeking clarification of an ambiguous message—and they think nothing of passing on the rumors and half-baked ideas they receive when copied on an email.

If you want to communicate clearly with a minimum chance of misinterpretation or misunderstanding, emails and text messages are poor substitutes for face-to-face problem solving and decision-making.

Chapter 10 — Conflict

Conflict is a normal result of what happens when people with different interests work together—so much so that we typically spend 25% of each day dealing with it. Under antagonistic conditions, it is not uncommon for that figure to rise as high as 60%.

Managers are frequently surveyed to determine their training and development needs. Typically, their responses suggest that conflict is a topic of growing importance. One survey, conducted by the American Management Association (AMA), rated conflict management "as a topic of equal or slightly higher importance than planning, communication, motivation, and decision-making." The AMA findings also suggested that ability to manage conflict would become increasingly important in years to come—a prediction that has certainly been proven true.

If your coworkers are not provided with a functional method for resolving their differences, they will soon have difficulty working together. It does not take long for such disagreements to erode respect between individuals.

Leaders are often frustrated by their inability to settle workplace differences between their followers. Usually they work around conflict, believing resolution to be impossible. They have come to view the process of conflict resolution as a situation fraught with potential disaster. They believe also that attempting to manage conflict inevitably diverts energy, destroys morale, polarizes groups, and deepens differences—in other words, it encourages dysfunctional behavior.

It is common in most organizational cultures for leaders and followers to have negative perceptions of conflict. Typically, this belief is based upon personal experiences where varying points of view were not allowed. They harbor a belief that conflict is destructive and should therefore be avoided. As a result, they lack an appreciation for the creative aspects of blending different perspectives.

Those who hold this belief fail to realize that a well-managed conflict-resolution process can uncover buried issues, open up new ideas, and inspire innovation. When properly managed, conflict can provide a natural source for creativity, problem solving, and team building.

Sources Of Conflict

So... how does one develop a viable conflict resolution strategy? Start by understanding the dynamics involved in organizational conflict. Most conflicts start small, but become magnified in a culture of ambiguity, inconsistency, and uncertainty—an atmosphere prevalent within dysfunctional organizations that lack proper planning and decision-making processes.

The majority of organizational conflicts can be traced to questions of authority and responsibility, competition for limited resources, lack of accountability, unclear work priorities, loosely enforced policies, lack of ethics and values, vague or unclear communications, and differing work behavioral expectations.

Doers frequently have different expectations for themselves than they have for their co-workers—and their co-workers have for them. When expectations differ, disagreements are inevitable. The varied ways in which people approach their jobs—how they obtain the desired results—also create conflict. Differing styles of work behavior can trigger what are perhaps the most common conflicts in the workplace: personality clashes.

It does not take long for such disagreements to erode respect between people and between work units. So, how does one get people with dissimilar behavioral patterns to work together? The answer is to capitalize on the unique traits each behavioral style brings to the relationship. Determining whose viewpoint should prevail only provokes the dispute and fails to resolve the issue. When the emphasis is placed on who is right or who is wrong, conflict becomes "you against me," which leads to disruption and dysfunction.

A landmark study by Aamodt and Wilson at the University of Arkansas demonstrated the importance of group composition to group dynamics. The researchers defined the purpose of the study as, "To investigate the effects of group composition, based upon trait homogeneity-heterogeneity, on group problem-solving ability." Subjects were assigned to two groupings: one grouping was homogeneous, meaning all had similar traits, and one grouping was heterogeneous, meaning each person had dissimilar traits. Both groupings were given the same series of structured and unstructured tasks to resolve. Analysis of the results showed a significant difference in the quality of the outcomes produced by the heterogeneous groups.

The Results and Discussion section of the study stated, "The results strongly suggest that group heterogeneity may lead to better group performance than that of groups composed of homogeneous individuals. This finding, especially if replicated with a larger number of groups and with different types of tasks, supports the notion of team building in organizations."

The University of Arkansas study concluded that groups of people with differing personalities performed better than groups where everyone was the same. The underlying assumption is that these heterogeneous groups were able to capitalize on their differences. In other words, they found a way to resolve conflict or at least keep conflict from blocking their ability to work together.

Many unfounded assumptions have been made regarding the value of working together in groups, one being that people will always perform better in a group than they will individually. Not so! This only happens when there is a means of resolving differences between the individuals in the group, and between that group and other groups.

No-No List

It is common practice to avoid openly discussing your most serious conflicts, wishing to avoid the potentially negative consequences of disclosing your feelings. During your formative years, parents and teachers, serving as social guides, warned you against the perils of outspokenness. Their teachings emphasized the value of cooperation and the importance of not making waves.

Repetitive injunctions like, "If you can't say something nice, don't say anything at all." clearly warned us to keep our mouths closed in front of others—or at least to be careful what we said. The supposed intention of these childhood admonitions was to teach us not to offend people. It is more likely that the underlying purpose was to keep us from embarrassing our elders in front of their friends.

The condemnation that followed an innocent childhood disclosure of a family secret in front of guests is not something we forget easily. That lesson, once taught, is seldom forgotten. As adults, we still tend to avoid discussing issues that might provoke retribution. But as we form into teams, with our different styles, values, and behavioral patterns, and try to work together, there are bound to be conflicts. Acting as though a conflict does not exist—treating it as a "no-no"—erects barriers. If a work unit does not have a method for resolving conflict, that unit will eventually become dysfunctional and unable to perform as expected.

This effect is cumulative: there is a direct correlation between the length of the no-no list and the level of dysfunction within a work unit. That is, the longer the list, the greater the dysfunction between and among individual team members. It is important to understand how unresolved conflict, stored internally on the no-no list, relates to the development of organizational dysfunction. You may recall from the review of the formation of dysfunction in Chapter 9, it takes place in four stages:

First, ambiguity is not questioned.

For example, a vague directive has an employee being presented with two ways of doing something, but she does not point this out or ask for the conflict to be clarified.

Second, inconsistencies are ignored.

For instance, a rule is followed by some people but ignored by others, yet nothing happens to the violators.

Third, ambiguities and inconsistencies are undiscussable.

It becomes politically incorrect to openly talk about the existence of ambiguities and inconsistencies. People will not risk getting themselves or others into trouble by sharing real issues and telling the truth.

Fourth, undiscussability is undiscussable.

Team members ignore the fact that ambiguities and inconsistencies are not openly discussed. Silence during meetings not only implies that conflicting issues do not exist; it also signals that the absence of open discussion about the differences will not be talked about either.

A no-no list exists when team members avoid open discussions of relevant issues. Instead, they get bogged down in never-ending debates over unimportant issues like copy machine usage, iPhones ringing in meetings, office furniture, the computer system, and who should be invited to the office party.

Over-reaction to a simple mistake is another clue that bigger, unstated conflicts are buried on the no-no list. The longer the list gets, the more tense and anxious people become to avoid discussing conflicts for fear of a major blow-up. A long list also indicates the nonexistence of an effective conflict-resolution strategy. Doers find it hard to thrive in the tension-filled environment that inevitably results from unresolved conflict.

Conflict Sequencing

Items are placed on the no-no list whenever they become a source of unresolved conflict. For example, two employees decided to air their differences in a good faith attempt to resolve a problem. Unfortunately, they get in to an argument where both hold firm to their position. The participants are discouraged. Rather than being resolved, their differences have been magnified instead.

Disappointing experiences, especially where there is an emotional investment, leave negative impressions. So regardless of how important it might be for this conflict to get resolved, it is not likely that these two folks will bring it up again—certainly not on their own.

That issue settles onto the no-no list. As time passes, other unit members will get into discussions of their differences and experience similar outcomes. The team's no-no list will lengthen, mistrust will set in and a dysfunctional norm is established. Unless the pattern changes, the list will continue to grow until the unit chokes on the volume of indigestible issues.

Remember, the goal is not to resolve conflict, but to manage it. Conflict is a natural source of creativity and the root element of synergy. Only when conflict is hidden or stored on the no-no list does it serve no useful purpose.

Unresolved conflicts inhibit collective efforts by keeping people from exploring mutually supported alternatives. A formal program brings conflict into a public forum where it can be properly examined and fully understood.

The purpose of conflict management is to work through the entire no-no list sequentially. Typically, the heaviest conflict issues are at the top the list. Not only did they surface first, but they have also been there so long that they have taken on additional weight. More recent items—which have been tacked onto the bottom of the list—are much less significant. Start at the bottom with the least significant issues and work upwards through the list. This is called conflict sequencing. Understanding how conflict-sequencing works will help the team get to those deeper issues that are blocking their work.

Working through the conflict sequence in this manner makes it more likely that subsequent conflicts will be resolved more easily and with a higher level of satisfaction. Conflict sequencing opens up communication between participants and thus enables them to get to the deeper issues on the no-no list. If an issue cannot be resolved, then it is set aside so as not to stop the conflict sequence. That issue may be revisited once progress has been made on other issues.

Here is an example of how conflict sequencing was applied to a ninety-year old family owned firm that was struggling to hand over directorship to the next generation. The first hint of how difficult this challenge might be came during the introductory meeting with the next generation of aspiring leaders who were in line to take their place on the board of directors.

Just as I was about to go around the conference table asking for the names and titles of those present an angry voice shouted, "Who stole my pen?" The retort was quick, "It's the company's pen, not yours!" The first angry voice rebounded, "My name is on it. You can't just take my things without asking." Back came the disclaimer, "I don't need your permission. You're not my boss." Glancing at the pen in question I noticed a piece of white tape attached with a name written on it in bold letters.

This verbal battle escalated as others took sides or started arguments of their own. The blaming and faultfinding went back and forth across the table like a doubles Ping-Pong match. Apparently this was normal behavior, as no one other than me seemed disturbed by it.

As the arguments heated up the issues became personal and moved backward in time sequence. Their conflicts were longstanding, some going back to childhood. This had the potential for being the longest no-no list I had ever encountered.

They were not ready to listen to me, so seeing no point in wasting my time I stood up with the intention to leave. Someone noticed and asked where I was going. My reply, "To the Board of Directors meeting to give my report.

"What are you going to tell them?" came the challenge.

First, my report is intended to ensure the company's future is thoughtfully planned, purposefully directed, and skillfully executed. In order for this to happen in a timely manner I recommend that the Board search for directors from outside the family to fill the upcoming vacancies.

Second, I will suggest that the Board develop a succession plan for each family member who they feel has directorship potential.

Lastly, I will recommend that those family members not included in the succession plan be trained in the use of the Conflict Sequencing Model.

Now that I had their full attention I went on to explain that unless those assembled here were willing to search out the root cause of their interpersonal issues, nothing would happen to resolve their longstanding conflicts.

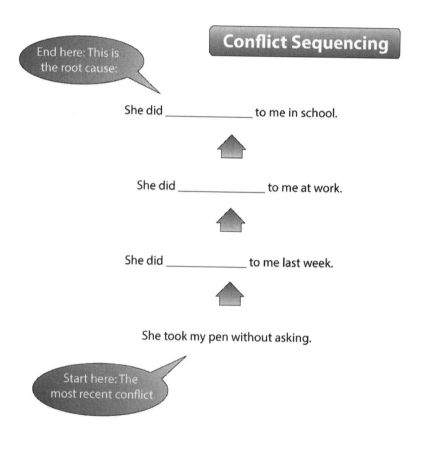

Figure 11 — Conflict Sequencing

Instead, they will keep track of how many points they can make by arguing with each other. This is known as the "zero sum" game—meaning that the side with the most points wins when the other side gives up or stops arguing.

The side that wins will not bring the issue up again for fear that the opposition has gathered the support of more powerful people further up the chain of command, and the losing side will not bring it up again for fear of another defeat. The issue is not resolved, but simply added to the no-no list. The winner gets a plus (+) and the loser gets a minus (-), the sum of which is zero (0).

If this game continues, the company gains nothing and becomes dysfunctional because the directors cannot resolve their differences without keeping score of the winners and losers. No organization can survive under the direction of leaders who focus only on being right.

The Conflict Sequence steps described below can be used by individuals or in teams using a facilitator.

1. Tracking

Begin tracking a conflict as soon as signs appear that it exists. Signs include raised eyebrows, caustic comments, unanswered requests, over reactions to minor issues. Discussions focused on who was right or wrong. People watch each other closely for reactions.

2. Building

Rather than dissipating, the conflict begins to grow. People will only talk about the issues surrounding the conflict in ambiguous terms and continue to ignore their misunderstandings. More people seem aware the conflict exists, even if they do not fully understand who or what is involved. They are beginning to either choose sides or distance themselves to avoid involvement.

The next three stages of the Conflict Sequence are the core of the process. They outline the necessary steps to get RID of the conflict and keep it from settling onto the no-no list. RID is an acronym standing for Recognizing, Identifying and Discussing.

3. Recognizing

Conflict is apparent, and the issues need to be brought out into the open. Choose a strategy that acknowledges the conflict, while suspending judgment as to who or what is right or wrong.

Make it clear what you are trying to accomplish. Share your objectives with key players and communicate your goals throughout the organization. Your purpose must be legitimate; for example, to improve quality, decrease turnover, build morale, or increase productivity.

Select a disinterested third-party to gather information from those directly involved.

4. Identifying

Pull the key players together to facilitate a non-judgmental examination of the issues underlying the conflict. Explain that you are providing an opportunity for people known to be in conflict to communicate within the security of a group session. Encourage antagonists to share the basis for their views. Emphasize that you value individual contributions, but that you do want a joint resolution.

Blend expectations by focusing on the vantage points that all participants have in the conflict. Ask them how it looks from where they sit. Encourage them to:

- Make a list of expectations for each one involved.
- Pinpoint the source of all unmet expectations.
- Identify the role of each player.
- Clarify the significance of each issue and determine the priority of resolving them.
- Openly declare your willingness to continue the process until a resolution is agreed upon.

5. Discussing

Have the key players define the conflict. Explain resolution techniques and negotiation methods, and then have them state their expectations of the process. Set the stage by documenting all attempts to resolve conflict.

Openly examine what worked and what did not. Record any unsuccessful experiences; these are opportunities to try again. Even if a resolution did not occur, a major step was taken to get the conflict off the no-no list and out into the open. A basis for trust was established, thus making future conflict resolution less stressful for all parties.

Encourage those who experienced minor success to continue to work through the process. Direct those with unresolved conflicts to focus on what needs to change rather than who needs to change.

By this point people should understand how the conflict has evolved and be ready to select a technique for resolution. Have them agree on a means of resolution, appoint neutral monitors, establish time lines, and begin working on the resolution.

6. Reconciling

This is the last stage of the Conflict Sequence Model. It calls for re-evaluation of the conflict, its underlying issues, and its proposed resolution. Note the time lines established in Step 5 above.

Informally poll the key players and the neutral monitors and use the information they share to answer the following questions:

- Have the parties settled their differences?
- Are there any hurt feelings?
- Is any restitution necessary?
- Are the expectations of those involved being met?
- What lessons have been learned?
- How should these lessons apply to future conflict?

If further action is warranted, pull the involved parties together and revisit the sequencing steps to address any unresolved aspects of the original conflict. Help them understand that resolution is vital and that they are responsible for achieving it.

The Importance Of Resolving Differences

When evaluating the need for conflict resolution, consider the fact that productivity is directly related to job satisfaction. As satisfaction drops, so does productivity. Personality conflicts, poor people interactions, and management disinterest are among the primary causes of workplace friction.

Without the benefits of a conflict resolution process, work-centered conflicts will damage relationships and drive people apart. Research shows that the Doers who are the most competent workers will be the first to flee a hostile workplace. Consider what it would mean, should your high achievers leave to seek harmony elsewhere.

Under achievers fear being wrong or worry that their views are different. They see conflict as disapproval of their performance. To them, conflict is two-sided. They think, "If I'm right, then you must be wrong, but if the reverse is true, I don't want to know about it."

A conflict resolution strategy can be adapted to meet the needs of any organization, work unit or individual. Most of us are reluctant to listen to opposing views because we fear we will hear something that might downgrade our position, hurt our feelings, or make us feel inadequate. In order to resolve conflict, this kind of thinking needs to change.

The ultimate goal of conflict management is to search for permanent solutions. Quick fixes do not last and need to be developed into long-lasting settlements. A closer look may reveal some of the deeper issues still festering. When given an opportunity to reflect on old conflicts, people often admit dissatisfaction with their hasty acceptance of a quick fix.

Oftentimes, their first response was an evasive reaction. More discussion may be needed before a durable resolution is achieved. A productive resolution is often based on a blend of each person's expectations. By taking the time to facilitate a permanent solution you establish the basis for trust and commitment.

Training non-performers in conflict resolution places the responsibility for solving their problems on their shoulders and frees up the leader for more profitable tasks. When a leader resolves the conflict between followers, the resolution belongs to the leader. The followers will continue to expect him or her to act as judge, which is time-consuming, unproductive, and dysfunctional. Those being judged have nothing vested in the decision, so they do not feel responsible for either the problem or the means of ending it. More importantly, judgment fosters disagreement, disrespect, and disconnection.

Build a stronger sense of unity by avoiding the use of judgmental or disconnecting phrases such as:

"I disagree."

"You're wrong."

"Everyone knows... "

"I may be wrong, but..."

"Correct me if I'm wrong."

"What you don't understand is..."

Such phrases set boundaries and discourage the further exploration of differing points of view, particularly from underachievers. Since the purpose of conflict management is to collect as many views as possible, the goal is to draw both high achievers and non-performers into the process so that they feel accepted as a team member and connected to the resolution process.

The way to encourage connection, especially when there are strong people with divergent opinions involved, is to use phrases like:

"Yes."

"And..."

"Or..."

"Okay."

"Good."

"Thanks."

The use of connecting words make those willing to speak out feel that their contributions have been recognized. Underachievers are more likely to change their position and be more open to others when they know their current view has been acknowledged.

Managing conflict in a dysfunctional workplace involves selecting an appropriate resolution process, building a strategy that meets the team's needs, blending individual expectations, setting the stage for negotiation, and searching for permanent solutions.

Those who work together must learn how to express their concerns, ask difficult questions, and face the core issues that are driving them apart rather than pulling them together. Without an effective conflict management strategy, no work unit can reach very high. Remember, if you do not manage conflict, conflict will manage you.

Chapter 11 — Change

In a progressive organization, long-term success is achieved by providing the workforce with opportunities to develop beyond its current capabilities. Aligning Doer potential with the future needs of the company is what sustains growth.

As time passes and customer demands shift, leaders and followers alike must accept that their jobs will need to be accomplished differently—that means change.

Change means that some of the forthcoming duties and responsibilities will be beyond the knowledge, skills, and abilities of the current workforce. If an organization fails to prepare its employees for the future, productivity will most certainly decline and dysfunction will set in.

Avoiding productivity declines means paying attention to how and where change enters an organization. The days of off-site planning retreats and long-term forecasts of market conditions are of very little use in today's market.

Change is much more subtle and thus more difficult to discern. If you miss it when it first slips into your world, it can appear to come on suddenly. The fact is you were looking for change in the wrong places. It is like placing a guard at the front door only to have the thief sneak in through the unlocked bedroom window.

Point Of Entry

The most logical place to start the search will depend upon the nature of change. Knowing where change begins to take shape in your industry can help you respond in a proactive, rather than a reactive, manner.

1) Change enters a service-oriented organization in the form of new or additional customer requests, concerns, and expectations. Employees who deal with the customers directly are the first to notice new demands and disappointments. Management must be open to employee suggestions for accommodating customer requests. Clues that changes may be necessary enter the service-oriented organization from the lower rather than the upper levels.

2) Change In the technology-driven enterprise comes in the form of requests for state-of-the-art equipment, software upgrades, and custom-tailored training. Relationships between providers and vendors change so fast that it is hard to keep track of which are still reliable sources. Frustrations mount as the first adapters accept the change faster than the status-quo-seekers. Ambiguity and inconsistency become constant sources of frustration at the mid-management level.

3) Educational institutions tend to ignore change until the public, through the political process, pressures the legislature to pass mandatory reforms. In response, educators hire other educators as consultants to confirm that reform is not necessary; claiming instead that what is needed are more classrooms, more equipment, and more money. Change, if it happens at

all, takes years; the modifications that do squeak through are usually too little and too late to have a measurable impact.

4) Governmental agencies are more accustomed to change than any other sector, since they are driven by legislation and therefore are constantly in a state of flux. The problem is that many changes are based upon political decisions that could be overturned by the next election. Seldom do career bureaucrats get excited about change. Instead, they hold fast to the status quo knowing that the latest push will not last long enough to make a difference in the way things work.

5) The health care industry either ignores change or is caught up in squabbles between advocates for patient costs and advances in patient care. Medical technology has forced health providers to change the way they think about medical economics. The turmoil is felt both inside and outside of the practice of medicine. Change creates a no- win situation for providers and patients.

Regardless of the nature of the change, Doers need to collectively examine old habits and prejudices, think in new ways, acquire additional skills, and prepare to do things differently.

Change provides an opportunity to question and compare current processes to future needs. This is also an opportunity to open up the current culture for examination and to determine if anything is out of alignment. If something is broken, now is the time to fix it.

Selecting A Change Strategy

Forcing people to change before they are ready is like asking a right-handed person to start using his or her left hand instead. Even if that person agrees to the change and begins the mental process of adapting the left hand to new uses, there would still be great resistance and frequent pain from the straining muscles until the desired level of dexterity was attained. Perhaps this is why many people view change as such a painful experience.

The vitality of any organization depends on its ability to change with minimum upheaval. Selecting the appropriate strategy makes the process of change less personal and more practical. It also puts the Doers in a better position to positively influence the way their coworkers respond.

An organization, just like an individual, will change when it is ready. The challenge is to get all work units prepared at the right time. Keep that thought in mind as you review the following strategies.

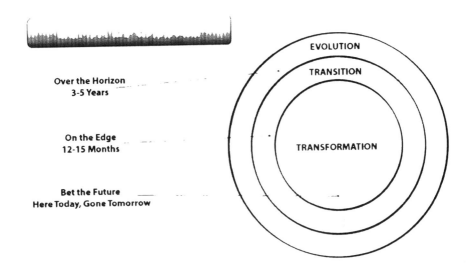

Over the Horizon
3-5 Years

On the Edge
12-15 Months

Bet the Future
Here Today, Gone Tomorrow

EVOLUTION

TRANSITION

TRANSFORMATION

Figure 12 — Depth of Change

Over the Horizon — This evolutionary strategy is also referred to as long range planning because it implies that things will be different 3-5 years from now. A long view allows plenty of time to absorb the potential effects of change before anything serious happens. Participants have time to consider how the change may affect them individually and collectively. Opportunities are provided for people to share their concerns with management. Periodically, the plans are modified and accommodations are made to ensure buy-in.

On the Edge — This pragmatic strategy is sometimes called transition planning. It has a fixed time frame with specific commencement and completion dates—usually measured in shorter increments—12 to 15 months is typical. The bottom line is brought clearly into focus as costs and profits are scrutinized. Attention is directed to the rate of return. Marginal products and services are dropped or put on hold. Efficiency experts reduce costs and eliminate waste. Performance expectations and productivity targets are aligned to match revenue forecasts. This strategy is frequently tied to the budget cycle, and it usually involves the entire organization.

Bet the Future - This disruptive strategy is euphemistically referred to as rightsizing, reorganizing, or restructuring. The purpose is immediate transformation—here today, gone tomorrow. Actions include drastic cutbacks, massive layoffs, and sudden branch closures. Whole industries are relocated, sometimes to other countries, in pursuit of lower costs. Usually kept under close wraps until the last minute, this strategy catches people by surprise and sends shock waves throughout the organization. When used to preserve what is still viable, the benefits can be immediate if the change is staged as a reformation.

How People React To Change

Generally, people react to change in three basic ways:

1) Proactive people are progressive in their approach to change. They tend to value innovation and respond positively to negative comments, difficult challenges, collective concerns, and personal criticisms. Most notable characteristics: anticipating change, making things happen, problem solving, and self-assessment.

2) Reactive people are negative about most things and tend to openly resist change in counterproductive ways. Their survival instinct is strong and they are quick to feel threatened. These individuals avoid responsibility and, when things go wrong, shift the blame to others. Most notable characteristics: finger

pointing, resistance, overt obstruction, spreading rumors, gossiping, and sabotage.

3) Inactive people are neutral toward growth and development, and they go along with change without enthusiasm. They avoid offending others by dodging serious issues and sidestepping commitments. They accept change only when they see it working. Most notable characteristics: fence sitting, limited approval, qualified support, and conditional agreements.

Watch closely next time a change is announced and you will notice that most people assume an inactive position while watching the struggle between the other two forces. They sit on the fence until they see evidence that management is serious and the change is actually taking shape.

That is why it is so important for change leaders not to give up at the first sign of resistance. If you truly believe that the change is necessary and worthwhile, then you must hang in there long enough for the fence sitters to see your resolve and join in supporting the change.

The Challenge Of Change

Full disclosure regarding the potential downside of change also exposes everyone to the truth about the challenge they are about to face. More importantly, it triggers the search for new tools and new ways to make change happen. Lastly, it generates a completely new set of critical questions like:

- Who will be in charge?
- Are we missing something?

- What is the new chain of command?
- Whose help are we going to need?
- What current resources are available?
- How are we going to get them involved?

Doers need answers to these questions before they are ready to start work on a new product. Thereafter when a new product is in the planning stage, Doers will immediately offer suggestions for how to improve the product or service as it develops.

You will know when this happens because their focus shifts from the past to the present with a view toward the future. They will start posing task-based questions like:

- What consequences will I face if I am unable to do the job required?
- If I need assistance, what resources are available to me, how do I acquire them?
- How much time do I have to reach an acceptable level of performance?
- How is what I am supposed to do now different from what I did before?

These questions must be addressed before the Doers are ready to embrace something new. If answers are not forthcoming, the Doers will not risk aligning themselves with a potential failure.

There also needs to be some collective dialogue around the subject of change itself; not just what is different, but how is this going to affect the Doers' ability to work together.

Once there is acceptance and understanding of what is expected, all you have to do as a change leader is keep the Doers informed as problems arise and praise them when they make the necessary adjustments.

Management Cannot Do It Alone

Organizational change is not just management's job. The Doers must also be involved through meaningful dialogue and purposeful planning.

The best way to engage them is to organize teams to realign the resources and redesign the workflow so that all updated products and services are more marketable.

Once the Doers are assembled in topic-teams, the next step is to pose a set of task oriented questions that are strategically centered on the change itself. Here are a few sample questions:

- What are potential barriers to success?
- What is not working that we need to fix or throw out?
- What is working that we want to be sure and not change?
- What are we doing that can be modified to support the proposed change?

When you ask task-based questions, Doers feel valued and new relationships will be constructed between work units. Doers need to support each other while they develop new skills and discover new ways of applying them.

Change is about examining old habits, thinking in new ways, acquiring additional skills, and preparing to do something different.

It is the only time that the future needs of the organization are called into question, opened up for examination, and carefully measured to determine if anything is out of alignment.

Change also provides Doers with a rare opportunity to consider the highest and best use of their collective abilities and to think about what they can do to make certain their organization remains competitive.

Keeping Participants Focused

Be forewarned that if you are not watchful, your well-intentioned effort to bring people together to develop strategies could easily turn in to a group therapy session.

In order to keep the griping and complaining to a minimum, provide an agenda with a list of task-focused questions. The purpose of these questions is to bring individuals together around a common issue.

- What can I do to help?
- How long will it take to get ready?
- What am I doing that is no longer necessary?
- What am I doing that I need to change or modify?
- Who is ready right now and who needs more time?

It is a truly marvelous thing to watch people walk into a problem-solving session angry, upset, and ready to fight, and within a short period shift their focus to how they can all contribute to make the place run better.

Leaders and followers put forth their best efforts when both are ready for change at the same time. Assessing who is ready helps prepare everyone for a good start.

The sample questions above are designed to bring people together around a common challenge. Such questions are neither critical nor judgmental; they simply open the door for meaningful dialogue. Once people get used to asking task-focused questions, they will purposefully frame additional questions in this new, helpful language.

It is gratifying to watch people shift their attitude toward change when they realize that it is not just about them, it is also about their organization undergoing a transition. You will know change is starting to take hold when participants are discussing the benefits of doing things the new way. It is at this point that the impending change takes on a life of its own and begins to unfold naturally.

Transition Management

Effective transition management requires a high degree of information sharing. Doers need to understand not only what is being communicated to them, but also what it means and what action they are expected to take as a result of what they are being told.

Organizational communication during a period of transition must focus on moving the Doers forward. When they trust the communication process they are more likely to believe that what they say matters, that they are important to the organization's success, that they have ideas worth listening to, and that they are valued for their individual contributions.

To ensure that the change goes as planned follow the Transition Guidelines below to create a receptive environment for large-scale change. The following list of activities needs to be worked into the daily routines and operational procedures of each impacted department.

- Define the terms and conditions of the changes that are about to occur.
- Identify individuals and groups who will be the most severely impacted.
- Monitor the collective flexibility and cultural dynamics of each department.
- Analyze the political implications of these changes.
- Identify the new skills required and provide educational programs.
- Provide coaching to management in leading people through change.
- Conduct interventions for work units most resistive to the transition.
- Structure the communication channels to ensure that people are informed.
- Form a Transition Monitoring Team (TMT).

Transition Monitoring Team

The Transition Monitoring Team's purpose is to facilitate upward communication during a period of change. The TMT has no decision making power and is not authorized to take any action without first conferring with upper management.

Meeting with a facilitator regularly, the TMT keeps track of what is happening to people and to processes as the company moves from where it is to where it wants to be.

The TMT consists of five to seven highly respected Doers from a cross section of the organization. These workers support the transition and are known to be trustworthy and reliable.

TMT Roles, Responsibilities & Relationships

- Demonstrates that management wants to know how things are going for people.
- Serves as a focal point to review planned changes before they are announced.
- Provides a point of ready access to the informal grapevine in order to address misunderstandings, correct misinformation, and counter unfounded rumors.

Performance Pathway Model

As you can surmise from the number of guidelines there is much involved in the process of leading people through change. When those impacted directly can see what it means to them, they are more likely to support it. The leadership challenge is to show every follower what the change looks like, so he or she can understand, appreciate, and accept what the leader has in mind.

The Performance Pathway Model brings the transition process into visual perspective by showing key factors that collectively influence job performance. The performance pathway begins with the individual, moves outward over a time line, and ends with a measurable outcome. It is designed as a visual aide to assist leaders in defining those factors that negatively impact the performance of their followers during a period of transition. The model is most helpful in isolating unproductive work behaviors.

Before we get started, take a moment and think of one or two followers involved in a transition whose work performance could use a booster shot right about now. Keep those people fixed in your mind as you learn how to apply the model in your workplace. Or if you prefer, think about applying the model to your own situation.

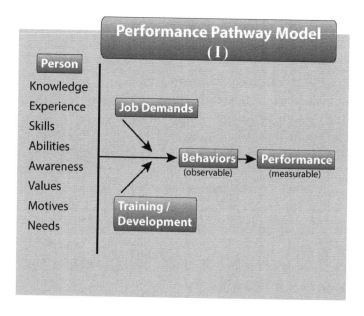

Figure 12 — Performance Pathway Model

Person

Individuals bring many traits and characteristics with them to the job. Some are desirable (functional) while others are undesirable (dysfunctional). The Person section of the model identifies eight factors, which can impact on-the-job performance. As individuals grow accustomed to the job, these essential factors tend to change over time.

For a Doer these factors change in positive ways. For example, their knowledge increases, their experience broadens, their skills develop, their abilities improve, their awareness grows, their motives strengthen, their needs expand, and their values deepen. Such a person is ready for change and will easily adjust to whatever comes his or her way.

Underachievers bring these same traits to the job, but unlike the Doers, they are looking for the status quo rather than upgrades or improvement. Typically, it takes them longer to get accustomed to the job. Meanwhile, they are searching for the minimum acceptable requirements and not thinking about raising their level of performance. Thus, the last thing they want to undergo is a transition.

Job demands

These are the conditions under which the Person is expected to perform the job. Unlike a job description, which lists tasks and duties, job demands define work in terms of past, present, and future expectations. For example: was the person hired or promoted into the position because of his or her past job performance, present job requirements, or future job potential?

A Doer would relish the opportunity for advancement and greater responsibility while a status quo seeker in the same job would be threatened by an increase in job demands. The underachiever would be content with a job that never changed, while a Doer would and does get bored without opportunities for growth and development.

Training/development

Training relates to immediate, short-term upgrades and improvements. Development has an evolutionary focus related to future growth and long-term potential. The maintenance of individual skill levels is determined by the organization's training and development philosophy. For example, if the philosophy is to hire or promote people who are fully trained and ready to perform, emphasis must be placed on the recruitment and selection processes. Under this hiring strategy, higher levels of performance are expected in a shorter period of time. On the other hand, if the strategy is to train and develop people on the job, performance expectations are lower and people are given more time to get it right.

Behaviors

Actions people take in response to their work environment are observable; people react to conditions in functional and dysfunctional ways. Job related behaviors, if observed carefully, can provide the leader with the first clue that people are accepting or rejecting change. For example, Doers can be seen moving forward, trying new things, and making change happen while status quo seekers are holding back, avoiding anything new, and reverting to the old ways if not closely supervised.

Performance

Performance is the measurable outcome of the interactions between the Person, Job Demands, Training/Development, and Behaviors. Here at the end of the pathway is where the leader discovers what is working and what is not. The results of all your plans are reflected at this final stage. But, this is also a beginning—a place to start again. Armed with the results, the leader is now in position to show the low performers and underachievers how to retrace their steps and target specific areas for improvement. They will benefit by walking through the model step by step while the leader points out where, what, and how they can do better next time.

Strategic Application

High performance is sustained by maintaining a balance between Job Demands and Training/Development. This means that education in some form is provided in anticipation of future job changes. New elements are introduced to the job only when employees demonstrate confidence in their current skills and abilities.

It makes no sense to wait until performance declines before providing training. Underachievers are reluctant to admit they do not know how to do something, which means it will be up to the leader to discover their weak spots and keep their job skills current.

Continuously assessing future job demands and then providing developmental opportunities for those working beyond their capabilities is the key to long-term growth. Keeping track of current performance is important, but knowing each person's potential is even more critical.

As time passes and job demands change, followers accept that at some point in the future things will need to be done differently. However, if forthcoming duties and responsibilities are beyond their knowledge, skills, and abilities, they will be affected negatively, and the pathway will be driven downward— resulting in a performance loss as depicted in Figure 13.

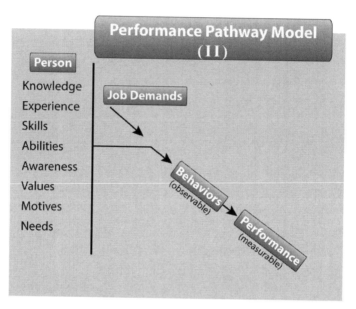

Figure 13 — Performance Pathway Model II

In a dysfunctional scenario, action is taken after the fact—belatedly providing training to those most negatively affected by the change in job demands. Rather than remedy a bad situation, this training may simply escalate the tension. Why? Unless the purpose of the training is made clear, a major clash in expectations is bound to occur between the leader and the impacted follower.

The leader will expect performance to improve, while the follower is expecting to achieve equilibrium— to return to the pre-change level of performance. If the post-change performance does not improve after the training, the leader decries the waste of time and money, and the follower gets a poor performance evaluation. It is no wonder, then, that change brings about fear in people.

There is wisdom in the saying: "The certainty of misery is better than the misery of uncertainty." People would prefer to know in advance how change might impact them—the bad with the good. In a functional scenario, followers are prepared for the change in advance.

If leaders want positive acceptance of change, they should hold frequent meetings, publish charts, graphs, plans, and share their view of what is about to happen. It is up to the leader to create a vision of what the future looks like in the minds of those most impacted by the change. Training people to prepare for change will affect their behavior positively and drive the pathway upward—resulting in a performance gain as depicted in Figure 14.

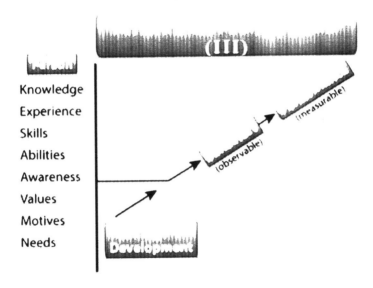

Figure 14 — Performance Pathway Model III

Chapter 12 — Expectations

How often have you found yourself in a situation where your expectations were not met? You could probably name quite a few. For the sake of discussion, consider the following hypothetical situation:

You purchase tickets for a concert performance of your favorite musical group—What are your expectations? What has to happen to make the time and expense worthwhile?

Fast forward to the end of the performance. Have your expectations been met? If so, you are delighted and consider the price of the tickets to be money well spent. If on the other hand you were disappointed with the performance, you may experience what psychologists call an "ego bruise" whereby you accept the blame and "should" on yourself: "I should have known better; I should have saved my money; I should have stayed at home."

Those "should" messages keep coming until you realize that you are not the one at fault. Now the "should" shifts to where it belongs: with the musicians that failed to meet your expectations. They should have been better prepared. The tickets should have been less costly. They should refund your money. And so on until the list of "shoulds" is exhausted.

Unless the concert promoters do something quickly to change your mind, your feelings of disappointment and dissatisfaction will be permanently linked to that experience. Most likely, you will disassociate or disconnect yourself from the negative consequences so that it will never be repeated. Most likely also, you will tell all your friends and warn them not to go.

You may never get the opportunity to share your feelings with the promoters or the artists. So, they will never get a chance to offer you a better response and perhaps shift your feelings from negative to neutral or even to positive.

This same expectations-response comparison occurs between you and those with whom you live or work. If they meet your expectations, you view the relationship as positive and are eager to remain associated. If their responses are less than what you expected, you may wish to dissolve the relationship or disassociate yourself from them.

The reverse is true also. They are liable to disassociate or disconnect themselves from you because they did not get the response they were expecting. Unless there is a process that encourages the exploration of unmet expectations and unmatched responses, over time the relationship will become antagonistic and may fall apart, and the parties involved will never know the reason.

Fortunately, there is a way for you to share your dissatisfaction with the response from others that will rectify or resolve the negative feelings and restore harmony to the relationship.

The Expectation Model

Matching an expectation to a response is a process that unfolds in interconnected stages. An expectation is always followed by a response, whether positive, negative, or neutral. Even no response is a response. The link between an expectation and a response is measured by a time-line. The time ranges from the few minutes it takes to check your email, the weeks spent looking for a job, the years it takes to earn a degree or the decades involved in advancing your career.

The time-line from Expectation to Response is always going to be impacted by Situations, Behaviors, and Feelings. Sometimes very little of this process can be controlled once the expectations are set in motion. But an understanding of how each factor contributes to the relationship can help those involved to change either their expectation or their response, or both.

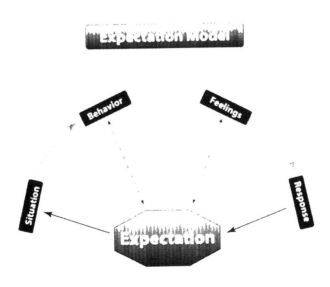

Figure 15 — Expectation Model

Expectation

Something is desired or anticipated, which in turn leads to a wide range of expectations. The objective is to consider all possible viewpoints. You know what you want to have happen. Ask yourself this: "What do those involved perceive their response to be? What do they expect to happen as a result of meeting your expectation? What do they expect from you in return?"

Providing satisfaction is predictive, if you are willing to take a broader outlook at the range of possibilities. Looking ahead you can "see" how the expectations of others might differ from yours and make the adjustments accordingly.

Situation

When underachievers get what they expect, they are pleased with themselves. If a situation arises that changes the outcome, count on them to hold someone else responsible. Walking them through the Expectation model will help them to understand how the current situation might affect the final outcome. The objective at this point is to either accept or modify those situations that are likely to prevent the response from matching the expectation.

Behavior

Most expectations are based on myopic self-interest— what is in it for you. This means that underachievers expect their leader to know what they need and to provide it without them having to express it. If the leaders response matches their expectations, they are supportive and behave positively. If it does not, they become antagonistic and complain that the leader should have given them what they wanted, or you should have tried harder to please them. In other words, they "should" on the leader and not on themselves.

Feelings

People are much happier in a work setting where they feel involved and important. That fact was made clear while observing teamwork among surgery teams in a large hospital. The situation unfolds as the nurses gather around the bulletin board just as the daily surgery schedule is posted. In addition to looking for room assignments, they are also checking to see which surgeon had been assigned to their team.

Nurses were overheard commenting on those doctors they liked and those they did not. They were very matter-of-fact about it: "Oh, I like him. Yuk, I don't like her." At first it appeared as if these selections were based on personality or gender, but such was not the case. When asked, the nurses said they liked those doctors who made their expectations known before the patient was brought in and throughout the surgical procedure. Keeping the nurses informed created a sense of inclusion within the operation room. Thus involved, the nurses could anticipate the needs of the surgeon and respond appropriately.

When similarly questioned, the surgeons who were "liked" also shared their likes and dislikes of certain nurses, and for much of the same reasons. When the nurses and surgeons shared their expectations and kept each other informed, the team was inspired to work in harmony. As a team they prepared for each operation with high expectations for themselves and, more importantly, for their patients.

When their expectations were met, both the nurses and surgeons were left with good feelings about working together. On those occasions where expectations were not met the entire operating room team felt disappointed, discouraged, or disillusioned. But rather than share their feelings and explore the situation they preferred instead to keep silent to avoid the potentially negative consequences of disclosure. Thereby placing their negative feelings regarding the situation on the "no-no list" described in Chapter 10.

Introducing the Expectation Model allowed each of the nurses and surgeons to express and discuss his or her negative feelings and unmet expectations without discomfort or embarrassment.

Response

One of the primary goals of effective leaders is to match their response to the expectations of their followers. Their secondary goal is to respond proactively to those situations where unmet expectations have developed. Their third goal is to either rectify unmet expectations or persuade their followers to accept an alternative response.

Obviously, responses can be either acceptable or unacceptable. When a follower's response meets the leaders expectation there is seldom cause for concern or need for reflection. The outcome is acceptable and needs no explanation as long as the follower agrees to provide that response when called upon to do so in the future.

When the outcome is unacceptable or negative from the leader's perspective, the follower needs to be made aware of the difference between what was expected and what he or she provided. This would be a great time for the leader to apply the Performance Management process presented in Chapter 8 in a search for solutions as to what the follower needs to do in the future to ensure he or she provides the right response.

The least threatening way to introduce Performance Management is to frame a set of questions in the form of a checklist that tracks the natural workflow. Then work through the checklist until the impacted follower can confidently answer yes to each point. Once this process is complete the follower will have a better understanding of the leader's expectations and is therefore prepared to respond in a way that matches them.

Fictitious Frontiers

Fictitious frontiers are elusive barriers that status quo seekers construct when they wish to put off doing something unpleasant or want to avoid dealing with a difficult problem. When they cannot come up with what is expected on time, they create a diversion in the hope of postponing the outcome. By extending their response time, they are trying to lower management's expectations.

Underachievers also try to extend the time line hoping to postpone or avoid the potentially negative consequence. They will strive to convince the supervisor to lower his or her expectations. This happens when a supervisor sets the goal so high that an underachiever feels he or she will be unable to measure up.

If the avoidance strategy fails to deter the supervisor, the non-performer might then attempt to extend the time line, hoping that the supervisor will either change his or her expectations or forget the original objective entirely. More likely, however, the supervisor does not forget, but instead gives the task to a Doer in order to get it done.

Repeatedly putting things off is a characteristic of those who are satisfied with the way things are. That is not to say that delaying an outcome is always unacceptable. There may be worthy reasons to extend a time line or drop a project altogether. Perhaps the additional time truly would result in a better or more improved response. But if the reason for the delay is suspicious, you may be dealing with a fictitious frontier.

One such example is called the "project completion syndrome." When a new project is launched, low performers respond by saying, "Let's wait until everything is known and all the resources have been accounted for before we get started."

"After the new year," is another example. You begin to hear that phrase in late October or early November. It picks up momentum as the season of holiday celebrations kicks into high gear. When you ask for a quick turn-around on a job, you get responses like, "Everyone will be busy with the holiday planning. Why don't I wait until after the new year?" Or, "It's too late to finish this before year's end. I'll start on it in January."

It is common practice for status quo seekers to keep a list of fictitious frontiers handy in the event they are threatened by the possibility of not matching the stated expectations. One way to separate a fictitious frontier from a real time impediment is to work through the Expectation Model with those who claim to be affected.

Do not hesitate to challenge whatever fictitious frontiers you come across. Events or occasions such as holidays, vacations, celebrations, promotional searches, personnel vacancies, equipment purchases, system upgrades, take-overs, reorganizations, mergers, and training programs are all likely candidates.

Evaluative Coaching

Clearly, the priority goal for every organization should be to honor the performance of its high achievers by improving the productivity of those whose expectations are set lower. Yet leaders often struggle with the concept of raising expectations. Finding ways to improve the productivity of underachievers is not an easy undertaking. It takes time, determination, understanding, and patience.

One way to accomplish this is to use Doers as peer coaches to expedite the training and development of their underperforming coworkers. Most likely you see yourself as a Doer or you would not have read this far. Therefore, you are already in position to become a peer coach even if that role has not officially been assigned.

Start by listing what you think the person you wish to coach might expect from you. Then share your expectations of them as a response to the coaching process. Jointly establishing performance management and process improvement objects as outlined in Chapter 8 would be a good place to start.

Consider how the desired responses look from his or her perspective. Identify which of the stated performance expectations are higher than his or hers. Only by collecting his or her point of view will the whole picture emerge. Do not be discouraged if those you wish to coach are hesitant to respond at first. Once you have done this a few times, those you coach will begin to understand what to expect.

Underachievers will need to find a way to share their individual expectations without fear of being judged or criticized. By focusing on their vantage points, the source of unmet expectations can be pinpointed. And with some evaluative coaching, they will be able to raise their sights.

Productive resolution must be based on a blend of expectations. The challenge is to find a way of coaching underachievers that will lead them to higher expectations and more satisfying responses. Evaluative coaching is a way to reach them in a nonthreatening manner.

Evaluative coaching is simply providing someone with an understanding of where they are, an awareness of where they need to be, and a perspective of what they need to change in order to meet the stated expectations.

A coach does not have to be someone higher up the chain of command. Doers often make the best coaches because they use information, expertise, and goodwill to inspire and motivate instead of authority, rewards, and discipline. Using positional influence results in compliance while the use of personal influence results in commitment.

Compliance may be an effective motivator for an underachiever wanting to keep his or her job, but it does not have the lasting affect of someone who is committed to improving his or her performance. This difference in strategies can best be seen in the Olympic games where the winning athletes are quick to express their gratitude for the tireless efforts of their coaches.

The coaching process begins by walking the subject through the Expectation Model so that he or she fully understands what lies ahead. The coach should have a sample list of recent responses that did not meet expectations as well as those that did.

First discuss the underachiever's expectations in those instances where he or she responded appropriately. Emphasize how what he or she did is valued and encourage more of the same. Then go over those situations where the response did not match the expectations. Try to determine what happened from the performer's point of view.

A good way to initiate the discussion without sounding judgmental or critical is to pose a neutral question like: "Help me understand why you believe your response matches what was expected?" The subject probably thinks that his response was exactly what was expected. This opens the door for an exploration of the reason for the difference. Take this opportunity to make him aware of what should have happened and what needs to change.

For example, the team needs to build collaborative relationships and the subject you are coaching prefers to work independently. The subject is probably not aware of the tenets of teamwork as described in Chapter 1, so you will need to help him or her understand that team members are expected to:

- Do what they do best as often as they can.
- Share what they know.
- Point out mistakes.
- Work together to solve problems.
- Focus energy toward a common purpose.

- Promote a positive image of the team.
- Sustain good working relationships.
- Encourage mutual exploration of conflict.
- Develop skills through self-education.
- Build an atmosphere of mutual trust.

Changing Responses

Workplace expectations stem from a lifelong exposure to societal injunctions at home and in school such as "don't make promises you can't keep," and "honesty is the best policy." Most of us grew up expecting everyone to know right from wrong and to do the right thing the right way for the right reason. We come away from childhood believing that we have the right to expect fair and equal treatment.

This is especially true for Doers who are easily discouraged when their achievements are not recognized. As Doers gain confidence in their power to influence results, their expectations will rise. Successful leaders must find ways to match organizational responses with the expectations of their high performers, or risk losing them.

In today's fast-paced, high-demand, competition-driven workplace, do not expect Doers to give you a second opportunity to address their problems. As the economy picks up momentum, they will have more choices. If you cannot meet their expectations, they will find someone who will.

The trend toward Doer satisfaction is already impacting private enterprises. Non-profit and nongovernment organizations throughout the world are facing this dilemma. The swelling momentum behind reinventing, reshaping, and reengineering will force all organizations to become more Doer-friendly. Review the list of retention factors in Chapter 8.

The most pressing leadership challenge is to keep the Doers satisfied long enough to raise the expectations of the status-quo seekers and underachievers. Once leaders understand the dynamics in play in the Expectation Model, they should be in a better position to do both.

Chapter 13 — Alignment

Downsizing, rightsizing, reengineering, reinventing—these are all internal alignments in response or reaction to external demands. As economic and social conditions continue to fluctuate, there will be continuing pressure put on organizations and the people they employ to be flexible, adaptive, and proactive. People in leadership roles will be expected to foresee the need for change and to make on-the-job adjustments without losing momentum.

Unfortunately, the introduction of change starts people guessing. It produces ambiguity and inconsistency—the building blocks of workplace dysfunction.

The exploration of these dynamics begins by taking a look at how organizational misalignment can have an impact on Doers and what they can do when it does.

An organization is structured in one of three basic forms. The resulting form is determined by four factors. The organization is functional when these factors described below are vertically aligned in the same column.

Purpose — defines the reason the organization exists.

Function — determines management's primary focus.

Relationship — describes how employees connect.

Problem — describes the issue facing the organization.

Organizational Forms

Study each organizational form and think about which one most closely describes your workplace. Be sure to make note of any current or potential misalignment. Even though you may not be in a position to do anything to realign the current form, later on we will discuss options and examine ways to cope with whatever misalignment you discover.

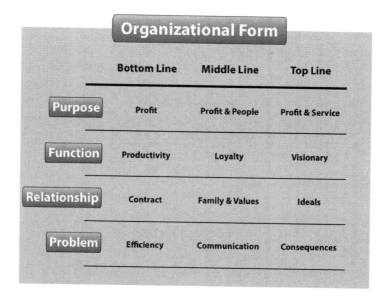

Organizational Form			
	Bottom Line	**Middle Line**	**Top Line**
Purpose	Profit	Profit & People	Profit & Service
Function	Productivity	Loyalty	Visionary
Relationship	Contract	Family & Values	Ideals
Problem	Efficiency	Communication	Consequences

Figure 16 — Organizational Form

Bottom Line Organization

Purpose — Profit

The bottom line organization has one driving purpose—to make a profit. Managers are charged with reducing costs and increasing revenue. Decisions are based on rate of return for the investors. New employees are hired and new equipment is purchased only after management demonstrates how such actions will improve profits.

Function — Productivity

The role of management is to raise the level of productivity without adding to the cost of the product or service. Staffing hours, production schedules, and distribution strategies are based on pushing more out the door. Emphasis is placed on speed and volume. Research and development are limited. Products and services are discontinued if they fail to cover the cost of production.

Relationship — Contract

Wages, vacations, benefits, job security, and promotions are based on how much each employee contributes to the bottom line. Employees are expected to be at work on time and to work hard while they are there. Discipline is tight and rules are strictly enforced. Overtime and layoffs are based on the needs of the organization. The performance appraisal and reward systems focus on continuous improvement.

Problem — Efficiency

Doing more with less is the common theme. Managers focus on eliminating mistakes and improving quality. High rates of employee turnover are expected. Employees are hired at entry level and trained on-the-job. Supervisors balance simultaneous demands for quality and quantity. Rewards are given for ideas and suggestions that improve the bottom line.

Middle Line Organization

Purpose — People & Profit

The middle line organization looks at people as the most important factor in generating revenue. Growth and development of the workforce are closely aligned with organizational objectives so that both will be together for the long term. The Human Resource Department is concerned with hiring people who fit into the organization's culture. Training and development are important recruiting and retention factors.

Function — Loyalty

Keeping employees happy and satisfying their needs are key features of the middle line organization. Building employee allegiance is important to management. The views and opinions of veteran employees are sought as part of the decision-making process. Those who have been with the organization the longest are highly respected as the pillars of the organization.

Relationships — Family

Employees are encouraged to view the organization as their extended family. Managers help people resolve personal and family related problems. Longevity awards and acknowledgment of birthdays, illnesses, deaths, marriages, and special anniversaries contribute to the family atmosphere. New hires participate in orientation programs designed to make them feel welcome and to acquaint them with the ways of the workplace family.

Problem — Communication

Keeping the workforce informed is a high priority for management. Employees expect notification of such things as safety hazards, production records, sales totals, and promotional opportunities to appear on bulletin boards and in organization sponsored newsletters. Managers use multiple communication media to provide frequent, adequate, timely, helpful, and accurate information.

Top Line Organization

Purpose — Service & Profit

Meeting the humanitarian needs of their local community is the primary purpose of the top line organization. The geographic area they serve supports their objectives through volunteering time and providing donations. Minimizing expenses maximizes incomes and profit. Managers spend time identifying new funding sources and planning new programs to serve larger populations.

Function — Visionary

The on going management challenge is to decide what the organization should do in the future. Extensive methods are used to gather information, conduct research, identify trends, and forecast growth opportunities and needs. Managers are pro-active innovators who frequently gather to discuss predictions, hopes, and preferences relating to the sustainability of their area of responsibility.

Relationship — Ideals

People are attracted to the top line organization because they want to make a difference in the lives of others. Employees believe that what they do is important to the community and contributes to the greater good. The opportunity to participate in a worthy cause is a strong motivator and contributes more to job satisfaction than do promotions or higher salaries.

Problem — Consequences

Decision makers come together frequently to identify and resolve important issues facing their organization. Before a proposal is considered, alternatives are explored in terms of what each might mean to the people involved. Management adheres to the principles of empowerment to ensure that everyone understands both the near and the long term consequences of their actions.

Organizational Misalignment

Layoffs, cutbacks, and plant closings are not new to the workplace. Realignments are a common practice during economic down turns, technological changeovers, and global market shifts. But in recent years it seems that organizational misalignment happens more frequently and is leaving a deeper, more negative impression.

One reason may be that most employees expect companies to function like middle line organizations. After all, they have been conditioned to expect employers to supply jobs to meet their needs. But in today's unpredictable market, employers are sometimes forced into becoming a bottom line organization just to survive.

There is nothing wrong with being a bottom line company, if it is properly aligned and clearly communicated. But when management says one thing, yet does another, that organization is misaligned and potentially dysfunctional.

For example, the CEO proclaims publicly that people are the firm's most important asset, even though the company hires mostly part-time employees, offers limited benefits, pays wages below prevailing rates, and lays people off when sales are down or business is slow.

Any organization pretending to be something it is not is misaligned and will eventually become dysfunctional. Bottom line counterfeits, masquerading as middle line companies, might promise long-term employment, growth opportunities, career planning, advanced training, and profit sharing. However, should their profit projections not hold up they quickly shift focus to the bottom line to save money and reduce costs. The longer term, higher skilled employees are the first to be let go because their wages are higher. This maneuver forces the remaining, less experienced employees to work longer and harder. Involuntary overtime goes up while performance goes down. Production declines because people are afraid to say anything for fear of losing their job.

These tactics are referred to in management jargon as "getting lean and mean," or "doing more with less." The net result in the short term might be an improved bottom line, but in the long term, it adds to the dysfunction in the workplace.

So, why should this be of interest to a Doer like you? At first it appears as if nothing can be done to change the existing situation. Not true—there are many actions you can take. In the first place just knowing what is causing the dysfunction should make you less likely to blame yourself. After all, you are not crazy—this stuff is really happening.

Additionally, by understanding the source of the dysfunction you will be able to help those around you who are having difficulty adjusting to it. Lastly, by recognizing the signs of creeping dysfunction you will know how to overcome it before it gains momentum.

It is amazing how fast a misaligned organization can move through the first two stages of dysfunction and get locked into Stage III where "ambiguities and inconsistencies are undiscussable." Should the misalignment continue it does not take long before Stage IV is reached where "undiscussability is undiscussable." The following are examples of real organizations heading for the fourth stage of dysfunction.

As you read these true life stories put yourself in the shoes of a Doer and think of how you might have reacted in the same circumstances. Think also about what problems you would have to face if these situations were to occur in your organization. It is a risk-free opportunity to practice with somebody else's problems. Who knows, someday you may find yourself in a similar situation and what you learn now might help you earn a promotion.

Example 1: Manufacturer

A large, growth-oriented company with thirty-one plants located worldwide and $1 billion in annual sales has for years posed as a middle line organization. The president of this family-owned business encouraged employees to seek increased responsibility with the promise of promotions and bonuses for those willing to take more responsibility. However, none of those who did so could explain what they did to earn their bonus and pay raises. Sometimes it was based on individual performance. Other times it was tied to sales or safety or customer satisfaction. For undisclosed reasons, the president was known to withhold or cut bonuses to an entire plant.

Some plant managers, who relocated at the president's urging, were left out of the bonus awards at their new location. The word got around to avoid start-ups because the company did not give bonuses or pay raises until a new plant turned a profit—an average of three years.

The employees at one of the most productive plants were expecting a big bonus because they had rated highest in every category in which a bonus had been previously awarded. The plant manager and his team were certain that they had all the options covered. But, it was not to be. That year there were no bonuses or raises for anyone anywhere in the company.

Instead, the president made a multimillion-dollar, tax-deductible contribution to his favorite charity. As the long term employees finally accepted the realization they were just part of the bottom line, morale plummeted throughout the corporation along with production.

Example 2: Health Care

As the local competition for registered nurses heated up, the bottom line thinkers at this middle line hospital came up with a revolutionary cost saving strategy. They proposed to lower the salaries of their staff nurses and, in return, provide 100% health insurance coverage. That way the hospital would come out ahead financially and the nurses would be "tied to the hospital for the long term."

The board of directors rationalized that if they cut base pay and then gave the nurses a more generous insurance plan than the competition, their staff nurses would have no reason to seek employment elsewhere.

Part two of this scheme included a generous cash sign-up bonus to attract nurses from the competing hospitals. This inducement, coupled with the increased benefits, was supposed to resolve the nursing shortage. It did not. Instead, it made the situation worse. The nurses felt less loyal to the hospital, not more. And, as professional caregivers, they strongly resented being treated like a commodity. As the bottom line came into focus, morale declined steadily and the nursing shortage grew worse.

Example 3: Service Provider

This nonprofit service provider had built a reputation as a top line organization. They had little difficulty attracting talented employees and top-notch managers who willingly accepted lower salaries in exchange for an opportunity to serve their community. That is until the newly elected board president, a bottom line business owner, convinced the board to set their sights higher.

According to his reasoning, the organization had to attract a higher caliber staff—and to do so, they must pay higher salaries. According to the wage and salary figures he introduced as evidence, this would require an immediate 20% increase. Despite warnings from the executive director and their accountant, the board, pressured by the president, approved the salary increases.

When the total costs were calculated the board found itself facing a huge budget deficit. The president looked again to the bottom line for the solution. The board would still raise the salaries, but to balance the budget, they would cut their matching contribution to the employee health insurance plan 50%.

The board was delighted with its efficiency. The employees were not. The higher pay rates increased their income taxes. Higher taxes coupled with higher insurance premiums resulted in a net loss of pay. The long-term executive director and several key staffers resigned in disgust. By making salaries and benefits an issue, the board had undermined the staff's motivation to serve.

According to the departing executive director, "They took away the specialness of working here." Following this chaotic episode, the organization became even more dysfunctional. The board president split the board into those who supported him and those who did not. More employees left. There are several lawsuits pending for back wages and unfair dismissals, and sadly, the pool of community volunteers all but disappeared. The greater good of the community no doubt suffered from the misalignment.

Successful Strategies

Organizational misalignment can also occur by design, when an organization purposefully realigns itself to face the challenge of change head-on. For example, in preparation for downsizing an organization may intentionally shift from the middle line to the bottom line while it decides how best to reduce costs and structure layoffs.

The following are examples of three organizations that purposefully realigned themselves in an effort to refocus their mission or redesign their organization. In each case, management intentionally engineered the change.

The organizations cited in the first and second examples were forced into realignment during a period of economic struggle. In the third example, an inspirational leader saw the need for change and realigned her organization to meet the challenge head on.

Example 1: Public Agency

An economic downturn can be particularly difficult for small towns that are dependent upon tourists for tax revenue. In this world famous resort city, the city council, city manager, and department heads had worked together for years and had become a very strong team. They were clearly a middle line organization in every aspect. The employees were long term and considered each other as members of one big family. Though everyone tried to maintain a positive attitude as the tourist trade continued to decline, it soon became evident that the current level of staffing would have to be reduced.

Department heads and members of the city council went into the community to explain the situation and gain support for service reductions. Management developed a plan to become a bottom line organization, at least while they dealt with the current budget shortfall. To minimize the dysfunction associated with the realignment, a Transition Monitoring Team was formed in accordance with the guidelines described in Chapter 11.

For the first time in the city's history, staffing was reduced. Those who lost their jobs were provided with assistance in locating new jobs in the community. It was a very painful experience, but it was handled as graciously as one could hope under the circumstances.

When asked how he felt after the layoffs were announced the city manager said: "It was like telling his four children that because he could only afford to keep three, one of them would have to find another family."

Example 2: Medical Enterprise

A few years ago, I had the privilege of consulting with a group of physicians who opened a truly unique medical center. It was not only the first such endeavor, but also the largest facility of its kind in the world. The founders were determined to build a top line organization that would have a world-class reputation for medical excellence, state-of-the-art technology, and unsurpassed diagnostic services. This was achieved through teamwork and constant training on the part of everyone concerned.

Since then, however, it was forced to downsize twice, eventually cutting the workforce almost in half. Without question, the decision makers shifted to the middle line first in an attempt to keep the "family together" because they truly cared about their employees. That reengineering effort kept them afloat for six more months.

But economic conditions worsened, and they were forced to shift to the bottom line in order to survive. A Transition Monitoring Team was formed to help the staff cope with the stress of losing 25% of their family during the first reduction. Six months later, the transition team was reformed to minimize the dysfunction when the second lay off impacted another 15% of the family. The organization was held together by sheer determination and the employees' desire to remain a top-line medical service provider. They still kept one eye on the bottom line, but are slowly moving toward the middle line again.

Example 3: Family **Services**

This is an example of an organization that started out as middle line, then shifted to bottom line and is currently striving to become top line. Not surprisingly, this series of realignments stirred up a lot of dysfunction. Not everyone wanted to leave the security of the small "family" that had worked together for many years. Under previous CEOs, the workload had increased, while the productivity had not. The staff blamed management and the managers criticized each other.

And then along came a new executive who said they could and would do better. She outlined her plans to enlarge the customer base and provide higher quality services. They had a mandate to fulfill and she was going to provide the vision to do it. In the process, she would raise the performance level of everyone in this organization.

Thus began a five-year commitment to improve quality and increase productivity. Within a short time they acquired state-of-the-art computers, the staff was nearly doubled, and the performance goals increased. Shifting from middle line to bottom line was easy. All they had to do was concentrate on efficiency and productivity.

Shifting focus to the top line has turned out to be much harder. Only the Doers embraced the notion of expanding the customer base to serve the greater community. Nearly a third of the workforce openly resisted the idea. The remaining majority waited to see who would provide the energy and leadership to move the organization forward.

A Transition Monitoring Team had been formed earlier on, but soon took on a more influential role as the Training Council, a powerful body responsible for all training and development within the organization. As the realignment continued, the Training Council provided new employee orientation programs, plus management coaching and team interventions to overcome both individual and organizational dysfunction in their workplace.

Making Adjustments

Many of us as children were led to believe that if we got good grades in school, we would find a good job with a good organization and earn a good living. Whenever the family gathered around the dinner table we heard how grandpa worked in the same job until he retired. My father retired after working thirty-seven years for the same organization. But now, as the worldwide economy shifts and organizations struggle to realign themselves to meet marketplace demands, the notion of steady employment with the same company does not ring true anymore.

Since Doers tend to draw their sense of purpose, meaning, and value from their workplace, the first place for them to look for signs of organizational dysfunction is within their sphere of influence. If they claim to be discouraged, disappointed, or disillusioned, yet cannot come up with specifics, they could be feeling the effects of a misalignment. Once the Doers recognize the symptoms, they can take steps to counter them.

Working together Doers can minimize the anxiety over change by helping their teammates make the appropriate adjustments.

Upper level management is responsible for communicating the purpose of change and their intentions for the future of the organization. Unfortunately, management can be distracted by the pressure of the situation and thus unaware of how quickly misalignment can create dysfunction. When communication from the upper levels is sparse, it is critical that the Doers interpret how these factors influence the way their coworkers are coping with the misalignment.

Adjusting to change can be rough for those who need a steady path to follow. In the event that an organization becomes misaligned, the Doers can still influence their teammates in a positive way. Should the organization subsequently become dysfunctional, the Doers may be the only people capable of providing a proper sense of relevance and purpose.

Chapter 14 — Strategy

Our propensity to create large organizations is stifling our ability to change direction without great upheaval. At a time when managers need to be fast, fluid, and flexible, they are holding on to an outmoded structural formula that is dragging them down. Today, size and strength are no longer attractive. It is true that there is strength in numbers, but it is also true that the bigger they are, the harder they are to change.

In a fast-paced, high-tech, consumer-driven marketplace, organizations with the longest history of success are the most vulnerable to buy-outs, mergers, or take-overs.

These current events give us a clue that we should be looking for alternative ways to respond to change. New strategies that hasten the collapse of outmoded and unresponsive systems are also needed. We must break away from the one-style-fits-all mentality.

If you can accept this concept, then you are ready to learn how to use a more strategically focused approach toward change, one that will be less disruptive and easier for people to manage. So, if it is that simple, why has it not been thought of before now?

Our current organizational theories have been around since the worldwide economic downturn of the 1930's. Those terrifying years of the Great Depression still influence the way we think today—probably more than we comprehend. Most senior executives in today's workforce received their education and training from people who lived through that horrific experience.

Sadly, here we are in the 21st Century still building fortress-like institutions to ward off another depression.

Before we examine alternate strategies, it will be helpful to dismantle the structure of a typical organization to see how it works and how it impacts the workforce. That way, you will understand how and why organizations become dysfunctional when they undergo change.

Under closer scrutiny, you can see that an organization is really made up of three subsystems as shown in Figure 17. These subsystems each have core values, membership restrictions, and definite boundaries, which can be heavily fortified and fiercely defended.

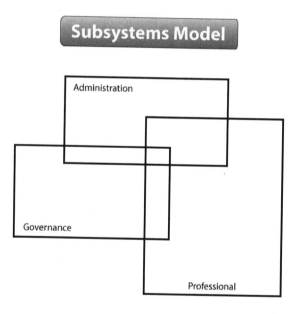

Figure 17 — Subsystems Model

If you cross one of these boundaries you will encounter what Annette Simmons calls "the strategic noncompliance game, one of 10 'territorial behaviors' that run rampant in the workplace." Her very practical guide *Territorial Games: Understanding & Ending Turf Wars at Work* is based on in-depth research into "dysfunctional territoriality." Simmons provides a much deeper look into these games than we can discuss here.

Organizational Subsystems

The size and influence of each subsystem depends to a great extent upon the nature of the organization and its stage of growth. For example, in a start-up company the professional subsystem would be the largest at first. But, as the organization grows, the administrative and governance subsystems will emerge and expand as the need for policies and procedures increase.

At the peak of an organization's life cycle, the professional subsystem will still be the largest, but the administrative subsystem will have the most influence. As the organization becomes rules-bound and slows down, the governance subsystem will enlarge and eventually dominate.

Before we look into how these subsystems interact within the larger organizational structure, a deeper look at how they function separately will be helpful.

Professional Subsystem

The professional subsystem is the most difficult to "see," but is the easiest to identify because it is the primary source of our on-the-job persona. For example, when a coworker is introduced for the first time, the second thing said about them, after their name, is what they do. This is frequently followed by where they are located in the building. Later, you are more likely to recall what this new employee does or where they work, than you are their name. Hence, organizational identity is derived from the type of work one does or by the company one keeps.

The professional subsystem is made up of the various skill sets necessary to keep the organization functional. Hospitals, for example, have doctors, nurses, technologists, and technicians plus a broad range of auxiliary services personnel each with a specific set of skills. Some of these skills are complex and require extensive training, licensing, and continuous practice to stay current. Most of these professionals belong to a group, association, society or union that offers external rewards and recognition unrelated to their organizational placement. Under adverse conditions such as those created by change, their primary allegiance is to their external connections rather than to the organization that employs them.

Administration Subsystem

The administration subsystem is the most visible. It can be seen on letterheads, marketing materials, office doors, campus maps, signposts, and telephone directories. In addition, it is felt whenever the discussion turns to personnel resources, space utilization, or fiscal responsibility. The administration subsystem keeps track of the wages and salaries for all employee classifications. Traditionally, personnel or human resources functions such as position descriptions, performance reviews, employment interviews, job vacancies, disciplinary actions, promotional opportunities and application guidelines are all part of the administration subsystem.

Governance Subsystem

The governance subsystem is all about compliance to rules, regulations, and policies. Typically visible in the form of boards, committees, commissions, and task forces where the law is officially interpreted and justice prevails. Sometimes the rules are changed without provocation or prior notification. Those who work in the governance subsystem presume that the other subsystems are paying close attention to their deliberations and determinations. Rule changes and policy modifications flow from the governance subsystem in a steady stream. Most people are unaware of the full impact this subsystem can have until they violate a rule or break a law. The power and influence of the governance subsystem can be rapidly expanded through connections to local, regional, national, and international authorities.

Subsystem Formation

The subsystems grow together naturally then pull apart as the organization undergoes transformation. Start-ups are primary examples of how subsystems are formed and subsequently become more or less influential as the organization grows.

Here is a closer look at one example.

This start-up was the brainchild of four highly regarded physicians who combined their individual practices to form a medical group to provide exceptional patient care at reasonable costs.

They acquired land, put up a building, and opened for business. Their vision was so inspiring that ten additional doctors agreed to invest and eventually join the group.

Things got off to a great start. Finding qualified staff was easy; job applications poured in. The group hired a very capable administrator and a topflight operations manager. Working side by side, these two selected and provided training for the bulk of the new staff.

The uniquely constructed building was divided into an interconnecting series of expandable medical suites that would be opened one at a time as patient flow increased. In theory it sounded great, in practice it was unwieldy and difficult to implement. At first the patient flow was low so the doctors had ample time to counsel and diagnose without feeling rushed. The slow pace gave the staff time to file records, greet patients, confirm appointments, check test results, and take medical histories without the usual pressure associated with a busy doctor's office. From all indications, it was a happy, stress-free workplace.

But as word spread that the doctors at this new medical practice spent time caring for patients, soon the influx of new patients overwhelmed the existing facilities. As patient flow increased, the staff in the main suite began to complain about increased workloads. In response, the operations manager pressured the administrator to open a second suite.

The group board of directors withheld approval, saying instead that a predetermined level of income must first be reached. All the while, new patients kept coming and the pressure mounted to do more with less.

Some of the doctors were able to keep up with the faster pace, but most fell behind. It soon became common for staff to stay overtime to address the patient backlog. The sudden increase in staffing overtime costs forced the group to open up a second suite. Everyone believed this action would solve the problem. It did not. It only set the stage for a repeat of the problems each time the patient load increased and another suite was opened.

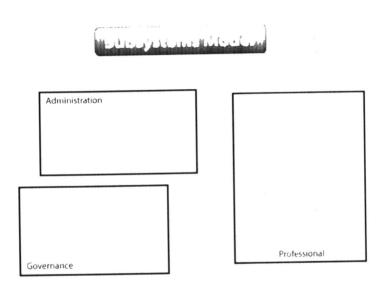

Figure 18 — Subsystems Model

A thoughtful review of Figure 18 provides a sense of how the organizational subsystems might have looked. Clearly the professional subsystem was detached and headed in its own direction. The administration subsystem existed mostly in the form of vendor contracts, supply inventories, bank statements, and billing records.

Other than the occasional memo from the board of directors or a periodic reminder of the need for continuing education requirements, there was very little evidence of the governance subsystem.

The operations manager complained about spending much of her day reacting to phone calls from confused staff asking for clarification. Turns out that when a new suite was opened the staff arrived to find no documentation, no job descriptions, no scheduling protocols, and nobody to train them so they called the administrator for help.

It was amazing how fast the dysfunction had set in—only a few months after the grand opening. The huge disparity between the professional subsystem and the other two subsystems appeared to be the cause. Once this became known, the board of directors decided to strengthen the two weaker subsystems right away.

The entire work force was pulled together to brainstorm solutions to the operational problems. Their first assignment was to assess the current level of dysfunction within each subsystem. The Doers were empowered to review the list of Dysfunctional Behaviors cited in Chapter 9 and make note of those that applied within their sphere of influence. The lists were collected, tallied, and then shared with the assembled group. The most frequently noted items were:

- Complex policies and procedures are initiated by memorandum.
- Requests for policy clarification are ignored.
- The search for the cause of a problem is personalized.
- People look for direction on how to act and react.

- Isolation keeps management from seeing what is happening.
- Inconsistent application of procedures is not challenged.

Armed with this new knowledge, the board could see what issues to address and where to start. A theme was needed that would define what they were about to do, one that would also engage the physician investors. The suggestion was made to treat the organization as they would a patient in need of urgent care. So a "medical emergency" was declared and immediate action was authorized.

First, they followed the transition management guidelines from Chapter 11 and formed a team of Doers to monitor the situation. Second, process improvement teams also made up of Doers were established to focus on the most poorly functioning processes. Third, a performance management task force again comprised of Doers was created to conduct a training needs assessment. Additional task forces were formed to develop policies, procedures, and protocols.

All teams were empowered to initiate changes they felt would resolve a problem, on the condition that they document their solutions and forwarded the list of actions to the administrator. It took only a few weeks to restore functionality and get the medical center running smoothly.

Subsystem Overlap

As you work your way through the section that follows, keep in mind the following three assumptions:

1) Change has become so rapid and unpredictable that more, not less; face-to-face interaction between Doers is needed to make intelligent strategic decisions.

2) Successful strategies for increasing sales, producing quality products, improving customer service, reducing costs, and finding better ways of working together will be based upon management's ability to engage the Doers in all subsystems.

3) When Doers have a hand in developing change strategies within their subsystem, they are much more likely to carry them out. Getting Doers involved early will reduce months, even years of potential resistance, misunderstanding, and low commitment later.

Notice in Figure 17 that all three subsystems overlap to some degree. Organizational functionality is determined by the size of this common area. The larger the overlap, the more functional the organization becomes. In other words, the more each subsystem's purpose is understood and supported, the more influence a Doer in one subsystem can have with the Doers in another.

As core beliefs become threatened, people tend to pull in their outstretched arms and put up their defenses. To keep them from pulling apart, Doers may have to reconnect with their counterparts in each subsystem. The strategy then, is for Doers to plug into all three subsystems thereby enlarging their sphere of influence.

Applying the traditional organization-wide approach to change will only force those with positional authority to increase performance demands or exercise more control. This means that in addition to managing day-to-day activities, a leader must also work with resistant followers in pressure situations, smooth hurt feelings, and overcome the resulting dysfunction; a tough assignment even under favorable conditions.

An organization is not structured to encourage innovation and creativity from within. Which is why Doers are often burdened with the task of planning and development— two complex tasks that are seldom appreciated.

Organization-wide changes are planned and professionally staffed in order to minimize the chance of failure. Why not do the same for changes to a subsystem? That is a good way to keep the subsystems in balance.

Doers are in the best position to clarify the authority, responsibility, and relationship issues within their respective subsystems. Additionally, by pooling their knowledge Doers can perform the following functions:

- Assess human resource productivity.
- Recognize, identify, and resolve systemic conflicts.
- Facilitate problem identification and resolution.
- Identify options and alternatives.
- Design implementation strategies.
- Determine training and development needs.
- Evaluate results and recommend changes.

Much like the medical enterprise in the preceding story, once the purpose of a change is clearly understood and formally accepted, Doers within the impacted subsystem become the primary advocates for implementation. Doers will then be in position to help others understand the change, which should also encourage support and promote more positive reactions.

Readiness

Previously, the subsystems were described as having core values, membership restrictions, and definite boundaries. It is these core values that determine the membership restrictions as well as define the boundaries of each subsystem. The strength of core values coupled with an assessment of readiness will determine how long it should take for a planned change to occur. Once both factors are considered, an appropriate strategy can be selected.

Managers struggle with organizational change for multiple reasons, some of which have already been covered. If the core values of a culture are deeply embedded, it will either take a long time or a great deal of pressure to bring about change. Conversely, if the core values are shallow or have not taken root, change can happen quickly. (See Depth of Change section Chapter 11.)

Just as individuals will change when they are ready, so will an organization change when its subsystems are ready. The challenge is to get the subsystems and the people who reside there ready to change at the same time.

Strategic Solutions

The future vitality of any workplace will depend upon its ability to change with minimum upheaval. By applying the methods described here, Doers can positively influence the way people react to change. Such proactivity will help coworkers face the challenge of change confidently.

A grassroots strategy is not as far-fetched as it sounds; it can and has been done. The following case study illustrates how a social service agency worked its way through a difficult and demanding transformational change by empowering its Doers to lead the way.

The director of a large social service agency had developed a national reputation for his innovative approach to automation at a time when computers were mostly used for record keeping. The Federal Government had just approved a major overhaul of the national welfare program, and included in the package were appropriations for pilot programs.

While the other directors pondered the implications, Mr. K was first in line at the state capital. He came away with a fully funded state-of-the-art computer system plus $9.5 million and the promise of more funds if the pilot program was running by the end of the fiscal year, which was nine months away.

His first challenge was to break the news to 2,000 employees. Not an easy task. Most employees were aware that the reform was coming and were not looking forward to the change. They had no idea their director had volunteered them as a national test site.

Mr. K broke the news to his department heads and program managers at a planning retreat. Based on past experience, he anticipated their negative reactions. True to form, there were plenty. The major complaint was directed at him for not letting them know in advance. After all, this would be a huge undertaking and they felt he should have consulted them. He admitted wanting to avoid the wasteful period of whining and complaining that accompanied changes in the past. Acutely aware of their history of resistance he decided this time to make the change first, and then deal with their reactions later.

The room erupted with loud denials. Mr. K listened for a while and then posed this question to the assembly: What would you have done if I had consulted you first?

One by one they put forth reason after reason for him not to take the risk with the whole nation watching. They did just what Mr. K predicted—tried to talk him out of it.

The loud grumbling went on for a while then faded to soft mumbling, as it became evident Mr. K was not changing his mind. Taking advantage of the lull, Mr. K stood up and headed for the exit. Just as he reached the door, he turned and pointed toward the group with a big grin and said in a loud commanding voice, "You're the management team, do something!" Then he left.

Startled at first, the group sat motionless. As they made eye contact with each other smiles began to break out around the tables. Soon, the room was filled with the energizing sounds of people ready to "do something."

Shortly thereafter they set about discussing the changes that must occur in the professional, administration, and governance subsystems, identifying those programs most affected by the change, and assessing their collective readiness. A few hours later, they sent for Mr. K and shared their plan with him. After a brief discussion and some procedural questions, he agreed to their proposal and scheduled a follow-up meeting to work out details.

Their scheme called for the formation of a transition management team to represent each subsystem. From a list of 125 volunteers, they picked thirty Doers to undergo extensive training in change management, responsibility charting, problem solving, and a variety of assessment techniques specifically tailored for subsystem transition.

They named themselves the Be Team. Their motto, "If it's going to Be, it's up to me," was emblazoned on T-shirts, lapel pins, and coffee mugs. Posters and notices appeared in hallways and on bulletin boards urging their coworkers to call the Be Team if they had any ideas or suggestions for solving a problem or providing better customer service.

Within a few months the Be Team's influence was felt throughout the agency. The transition was by no means easy and was not completed as planned. But it did change the way the agency did business and got them where they needed to be in time for it to make a meaningful difference. But what truly mattered to Mr. K and the Doers who lead the charge for change was the national acclamation and statewide recognition the agency received for completing the transition to the new welfare program as promised.

Chapter 15 — Failure

The booming decade of the '90s was a period of big deals and big profits. Eager investors flocked to seminars looking for high returns. "How-to" books filled the stores, while "get rich quick" gurus went city-to-city making converts.

If there was a downside, it was hard to spot. Reality and truth were hidden by growth and prosperity. This "go-go" period, as it was called, became the spawning ground for much of the workplace dysfunction we are facing today.

The most dynamic risk takers were called "champions." They kept pushing their ideas again and again until they found one that worked. But this reckless strategy also encouraged risk-taking without due diligence to the fallout from failure.

Had we focused less on the success stories of that period and paid more attention to the failures, we might have learned some valuable lessons. A couple of nationally known brand names come to mind: let's examine their downfall and see what might be learned.

First, the petroleum industry, which, thanks to the so called "energy crises," was riding the crest of an economic wave. Gulf Oil and Chevron were particularly well positioned in the rush to find more domestic oil. Gulf seized the opportunity to invest in additional federal offshore leases in the Gulf of Mexico. Chevron chose instead to take a different approach.

Rather than competing with Gulf in a bidding war for exploration rights, Chevron saved their cash and waited until Gulf had drilled more wells and located new deposits.

Satisfied that Gulf's cash reserves were too lean to defend against a take-over, Chevron bought the majority of its stock and took control. Within a matter of months Gulf dwindled in strength from several thousand employees to a mere handful of accountants and attorneys. Shortly thereafter, Gulf ceased to exist as a viable enterprise.

The top brass at Chevron no doubt worked on their take-over scheme in secret. But bits and pieces must have leaked. After all, employees from Chevron and Gulf lived in the same neighborhoods, shopped at the same markets, and took their kids to the same schools. They knew each other's problems and concerns. Gulf 's employees were bound to have heard rumblings of a take-over.

Suppose these rumblings had been brought to the attention of Gulf's decision makers. Would the information have been sufficient to alert management to the prospects of failure? Would they have believed what their employees were overhearing and then acted differently? Given the decision making style of that era, it is doubtful. Management would most likely have discounted any feedback from below that did not support their views.

The oil industry did not have exclusive claim to this top-down management style. If we look at the manufacturing sector, we find our second example: Singer. Over the years, the Singer brand sewing machine had become a standard household item. Singer had a well-known product and a solid hold on the market.

Management, expecting an increase in product demand, introduced a technologically advanced machine— one that automatically created blind hems and buttonholes and a host of various pattern stitches. Sales skyrocketed! Their investment paid off handsomely—for a while. But the good times did not last. By the end of the decade most of what Singer had going for it had been lost.

Why had Singer failed and what could we learn from it? They were victims of a powerful, unforeseen combination of social, economic, and technologic changes. As women entered the workforce in significant numbers, they had neither the time nor the inclination to sew at home. Simultaneously, department stores introduced ready-to-wear garments made to fit all sizes and dry cleaners offered tailoring services at affordable prices. It was not long before domestic sewing was on the decline—along with Singer's sales figures.

The experiences of Gulf and Singer are alike in many respects. Both companies were victims of unforeseen developments. Gulf became one of the earliest casualties of the financial strategy called a take-over. Singer lost its hold because of a shifting market.

These case studies serve as prime examples of the significant roles risk and feedback play in determining success and failure. Gulf did not have a feedback mechanism in place to allow input from inside the organization to reach the top. And, even if Singer's sales people had picked up on the downward buying trend the information was not communicated to management.

In both situations, management was entrenched in a corporate culture where the risks were high and the feedback low. Such a combination forces the decision makers to presume future events; since they have no way of tapping into information that could have helped them select better alternatives. (See Upward Voice in Chapter 3)

Lest you think the above examples are exceptions or they took place under unique circumstances, all you have to do is look around to see the same things happening in the high tech world today. The fortunes of Apple, Google, Oracle, Facebook, LinkedIn, Amazon, Twitter, HP, IBM, Microsoft, Dell and hundreds of lesser known hi-tech firms around the globe rise and fall almost daily. Some will learn from failure while others will not. Chances are a failure will occur in your workplace some day, and when it does, you will be one of the few that knows what to do.

Organizational Culture

When faced with a difficult decision you try to minimize the risk of being wrong by gathering as much information as you can. Sometimes you are pressed for time and therefore limited in the amount of information you can access. Making decisions with limited information is risky. When the degree of risk is high and you cannot get enough feedback to minimize it, you may put off making the decision until you have more information.

On the other hand, if the decision is of little consequence and the risk is low, you may act quickly, because in the long run, you are not that concerned about failure. Therefore, it is the degree of risk in combination with the amount of feedback that determines your behavior.

The same holds true in a corporate culture. The degree of risk in combination with the amount of feedback similarly determines an organization's reaction to failure. Both factors are represented by the Risk-Feedback Model depicted in Figure 19, which identifies four possible organizational cultures. In this model, risk relates to decision-making and feedback relates to information.

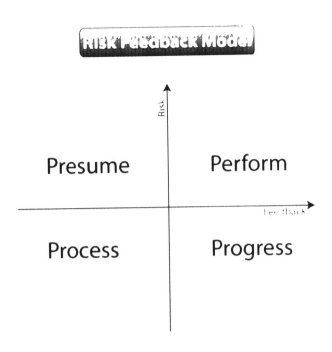

Risk Feedback Model

Presume   Perform

Risk

Feedback

Process   Progress

Figure 19 — Risk Feedback Model

The functionality of an organization depends upon how the Doers respond to failure, treat mistakes, service customers, handle complaints, create ideas, manage growth, and view success. As you review the description of each culture, make note of how that culture responds to failure and compare it to what goes on in your workplace.

Presume Culture (High Risk — Low Feedback)

- Crises are driven by high priorities at all levels.
- Employees move from one crisis to the next.
- People never know how well they are doing.
- Problems require bet-your-job decision-making.

- Opportunities for making a difference are few.
- Chances of continued success are limited.
- Failure is not tolerated and mistakes are costing.
- The norm is avoiding mistakes and making certain before you act.
- New ideas are modest improvements on what worked before.
- Innovation means it was pirated from another company.

Process Culture (Low Risk — Low Feedback)

- Limited risk is matched by infrequent feedback.
- Resistance to change is very strong.
- Failure is viewed as a career ending point.
- Once an idea fails there is no interest in trying it again.
- People keep track of their failures.
- New employees are warned not to upset the status quo.
- Customer Service is slow and unresponsive.
- Complaints are expected as part of the job.
- Change involves long periods of planning by many people.
- Ideas and suggestions are overly examined from every angle.
- The organizational norm is "don't rock the boat."

Progress Culture (Low Risk — High Feedback)

- Future plans and creative concepts are developed.
- Employees strive for success and take chances.
- There is ample time to develop and test new ideas.
- Developmental focus is both near and long term.
- Failure creates opportunities for testing alternatives.

- Information is available through easily assessable sources.
- Failures do not keep people from rising up and trying it again.
- People are fluid, moving often, changing positions and job duties.
- New projects are launched as soon as the pilot shows promise.
- Customers respond to personal attention and frequent contact.
- The more people put into the job, the more they get out of it.

Perform Culture (High Risk — High Feedback)

- Relationship between risk-taking and feedback is balanced.
- Sufficient information to fully understand the risk is available.
- Risk stimulates creative thinking and builds confidence.
- The best decisions are made when the competition hesitates.
- Everyone spreads out to look for new information.
- People know how to network with unique and varying sources.
- Change is the best way to sustain high performance.
- The goal is to keep ahead of the competition.
- Innovation means new ways to use old resources.
- Failure is expected and overlooked when it occurs.
- Customer response time is an important factor.
- New learning opportunities and creative processes are the norm.

The Meaning Of Failure

The Doer's challenge is to make present decisions with the greatest knowledge of their potential for future success, organize to carry out these decisions, and measure the results. In some cultures, meeting this challenge is simply a matter of matching the degree of risk with the right amount of feedback. In a dysfunctional organization, unfortunately, Doers are often deprived of information. In that scenario, the chances of failure increase each time they make an uninformed decision.

Functionality is determined by the way people react to failure. In a dysfunctional culture failure is not tolerated. In a functional culture failure is the price to be paid for success. The willingness of a Doer to risk depends upon his or her view of failure. Successful Doers understand the risk involved in any given situation and strive to overcome their fear of failure.

The fear of failure is constant in a dysfunctional organization. Confronting failure allows the Doers to learn from it and overcome it so it does not get in their way. It also helps leaders to mold their teams in a positive way, even when the surrounding organization is dysfunctional.

Of the four corporate cultures, the Presume Culture is the most prone to dysfunction. This is a tense culture, fast-paced and crisis-driven. People in it tend to be self-centered, close-minded, and mean-spirited. Succeeding in this culture is difficult, since both the risks and the chances of failure are equally high.

Underachievers are typically closed to feedback. Those that are open to it may not know where to look. The Gulf

258

Oil and Singer cases are examples of what can happen to an organization that gets stuck in a Presume Culture. Gulf and Singer increased their risk without upgrading their feedback process. Eventually, the lack of information did them in.

A few years ago I witnessed the dysfunctional aspects of a Presume Culture first hand. Late one afternoon during a management training session for a regional law enforcement agency in a remote area of central California a severe earthquake struck a nearby community.

Even though their emergency response teams were on call and only a few miles from the disaster, they failed to send help because the impacted district was not within their jurisdiction. Coincidently, it was quitting time so those not scheduled for routine patrol duty went home. Shortly after when the State of California Emergency Services Director's office called to declare an emergency and order immediate assistance, nobody was there to respond.

Fortunately, the quick thinking dispatcher was able to contact those bound for home and send them rushing to the scene. Once there, they did an excellent job. In fact, in a nice bit of irony, they were awarded a citation for their outstanding service.

The Process Culture is also dysfunctional because the people in it are nonreactive. This is a slack culture, slow moving, and crisis-resistant. The employees, while generally well intentioned, tend to be self-satisfied and close-minded. They do not respond in a timely manner and therefore discourage creative solutions to pressing problems. Getting people to change the way they do

259

things, even when such change is clearly advantageous and justifiable, takes a major effort.

In both the Process and Presume Cultures, underachievers will change but only when it is forced upon them. External demands put pressure on them to make decisions sooner than they would like. They do so reluctantly and without asking for additional feedback. Thus they risk being wrong more often, which in turn, increases their opportunity for failure. Given these circumstances, those who are already failing to meet minimum expectations feel threatened by change, as they fear it will demand more of them. Rather than looking forward, they start wishing for the good old days and talking about how great things used to be.

Locating Dysfunction

Start by sharing the Culture Model within your sphere of influence. Ask those most impacted to discuss the factors of risk and feedback and to describe how they as individuals and as a team react to failure. Add your view, and then lead a discussion on which culture best describes where they are now. If they pick the Perform or Progress Culture and you agree with that assessment, lead a discussion on what it will take to stay there.

The Progress Culture is a good place to be. The level of dysfunction is usually low and it is easier to catch at Stage I or II (see stages of dysfunction in Chapter 9). You may not have any reason to reshape this culture. However, if you want to move along on a developmental track, the Perform Culture is the best place to go next. To get there requires showing more initiative, which means the risk of failure may increase (see initiative levels in Chapter 8).

Before you decide to act independently, check to see what feedback is available within your sphere of influence so you can calculate the degree of risk. Once the information is collected and those who look to you for leadership have accepted the increased risk of failure, you are probably ready to move to the Perform Culture.

If everyone believes that they are in the Perform Culture, the challenge is to stay there. If they are satisfied that where they are is right where they need to be, use the Culture Model as a framework to determine how to deal with future risks.

Reviewing the model periodically can help those who seek your guidance to gain new insights while forging a sense of common values and purpose. As a result they should be able to clarify the specific steps needed to ensure a successful future even if the organization as a whole becomes dysfunctional.

If those within your influential sphere realize they are in a Presume or Process Culture, then the discussion should focus on how to change that situation. Since the level of dysfunction is most likely to be at Stage III where ambiguities and inconsistencies are undiscussable, a way must be found to open up the flow of information.

Since most people in a dysfunctional culture are not used to asking questions to obtain information, you may have to form the questions yourself. And, at first, you may even have to provide the answers. All is not lost however: one positive thing about working in a Presume or Process Culture is that if people do not have to act on the information provided to them, they will cheerfully listen to whatever their leader or coach has to say.

Strategic Components

As you begin to reshape your portion of the organization's culture, you may want to include the four strategic components below when formulating your plan. There are several ways to work your way through each of these components. You can do this on your own or involve those within your sphere of influence. If you chose this option, try to get them away from work for a few hours and ask them to respond to each of the following.

1) Environmental Opportunities - Identify those values and opinions related to what those within your sphere of influence might do. Start by asking them to share the events, developments, and trends they feel are currently impacting their collective efforts or forcing the need to change.

2) Interests and Desires - Determine a preferred culture based on what those within your sphere of influence want to do. Assess each player's view of the changes they feel need to be made. Each suggestion should be accompanied by a recommendation for what can be done to minimize the risk of failure.

3) Organizational Responsibility - Clarify both internal and external customer demands and expectations for what those within your sphere of influence should do. Determine how each player will work to ensure a successful outcome. Make a list of whose help and what resources will be needed. Decide how the required help and resources will be obtained.

4) Competence and Resources - Define the most successful course to take based on what those within

your sphere of influence will do. Set goals, establish time lines, determine priorities, and clarify the steps that need to be taken to ensure the planned changes are fully understood and supported.

The Doer's Dilemma

When surrounded by coworkers with negative attitudes, Doers may be tempted to withdraw or limit their involvement. They may also interpret the lack of recognition and appreciation as signs of failure. But, this may not be true.

Remember that by wanting to succeed in a Process or Presume Culture you are upsetting the status quo and going against an established norm. To avoid being caught up in the prevailing fear of risk and failure use the following principles to guide and sustain you:

Think of risk as a means of measuring the value of your commitment. You risk failure whenever you commit yourself to a dream or a vision. You risk losing support from others when you act on your own set of goals.

Look on failure as part of the learning process. You will fail many times. Examine the cause and avoid similar mistakes in the future. Adopt a no big deal philosophy. When one thing does not work the way you expected, do not give up—try something else.

Have a strong belief in your own personal worth and professional value. You may have faults, which others will quickly point out, but as a whole person no one is better than you. Feel good about yourself and trust that what you do is right for you.

Do not waste time with negative people. You will feel good about yourself when surrounded by people who hold you in high esteem. Do what you believe in and others will believe in you. Trust and support others and they will trust and support you.

Do not compromise yourself and your values. Hold yourself up and treat yourself well. You deserve it!

Working with people in a Process or Presume Culture is best done incrementally—a little bit more risk each time. Eventually those within your sphere of influence will understand that taking responsibility for their actions is not as risky as they thought. On those occasions when you do not have the time to explore the consequences of failure with your coworkers, go ahead and assume responsibility for the riskier decisions yourself. If they know you are willing to confront failure, they are more likely to follow your example in the future.

In the Process and Presume Cultures, people do not know what success looks like, so you may have to "picture it" for them. Make it clear that the current situation is unacceptable and that it must not continue as is. Help them understand why, and get them to accept the need for things to improve. Finally, state your goals and tell them what they can expect when the goals are reached.

Your biggest challenge as a Doer in a dysfunctional environment is to produce results that are recognized and appreciated. In a dysfunctional culture success is not an expectation; so do not rely on much support in your search for excellence.

If you do manage to make a difference, make sure your supervisor knows that it was you who did it. But do not be surprised if few of those around you acknowledge your achievements.

Three factors are key to maintaining a sense of personal worth in a dysfunctional culture:

1) There must be opportunities for you to make a positive difference.

2) There must be opportunities for you to grow personally and develop professionally.

3) There must be opportunities for you to do things that others cannot or will not do.

As long as all three factors are present, you may find satisfaction in your job even if your organization becomes or remains dysfunctional. However, if these opportunities diminish in value or cease to inspire you, it is likely that you can do no more. In that case, your next move would be to update your résumé and plan a graceful exit.

Appendix: A Case Study In Succession Planning

Job Announcement:

Exceptional Parents Unlimited (EPU), a nonprofit agency is seeking an Executive Director. Marion Karian, the founder and Executive Director is retiring.

Founder's Announcement:

I am planning to retire in January. It will be a difficult transition, but, as you know, we have been working toward it for several years. Our leadership team is very strong and as ready as they can be.

Background And History

Founded in 1976 by Marion M. Karian, EPU started as a support group for the parents of children with Down's syndrome. The name Exceptional Parents Unlimited was chosen because Marion wanted to provide services for the parents of children with all kinds of special needs. The concerns and efforts of these parents became EPU's foundation.

The mission of EPU is to strengthen and empower children and families facing extraordinary medical, developmental, and parenting challenges.

Over the years EPU developed a wide range of programs and services in response to the expressed needs of families. Currently the EPU Children's Center serves over 3,000 children and families with a budget of $7 million.

EPU has expanded beyond their original service area to become a national leader in providing and promoting comprehensive, family-centered services through five major programs.

EPU has a staff of more than 100 therapists and early childhood specialists. This staff includes a Chief Financial Officer, a Human Resources Director, a Development Director, a Director of Evaluation and Data, and five other program managers who make up the Executive Director's leadership team.

Families are most often referred to EPU by the hospital the child was born in or their pediatrician. A professional referral is not needed at EPU and any family member may call in a referral.

The programs at EPU are inclusive of the entire family: the child with special needs, their parents, and the child's siblings. Currently 800-900 children and family members are seen at the EPU Children's Center each week.

A fleet of 10 vans provides transportation to and from EPU for families within its service area. 20 home visitors meet weekly with up to 25 families in their homes.

Setting The Stage For Succession

As EPU approached its thirtieth anniversary in 2006 the founder began to consider the need to plan for her replacement. Once the word got out that she was thinking about retirement, long time sustainers, corporate sponsors, and major revenue sources all voiced their concerns regarding the need for sustainability without Marion at the helm.

A transition of this magnitude required the introduction and implementation of a future-focused planning model that would enable EPU staff to stay focused while the process of selecting and training a new executive director took place.

The Planning Wheel was introduced, as a purpose-driven model designed to identify, train and develop a core team of mentor-leaders who are empowered to reach across barriers and boundaries to ensure that sharing knowledge and teaching others becomes an instinctive part of their positional responsibilities.

The Planning Wheel facilitated the long-term development of Doers, which was beneficial to both the individual and the organization. Those Doers, with high potential who are selected for development are motivated to go the extra mile and stick around longer with the understanding that they have a future with EPU regardless of who takes the helm when the founder retires.

Using The Planning Wheel as their guide EPU leaders were better able to proactively respond to the increased demands on their scarce resources.

[Author note: As you ponder how best to apply the lessons from this case study, think first about how you would complete this statement: The purpose of the organization, department, division, or unit where I work is to _____.

If your response came quickly, can be explained easily, and fills you with hope, then you are in a workplace where the direction is clear and the future holds promise.

In that case The Planning Wheel model will help you to stay focused as you move competently and confidently toward the challenges that lie ahead.

If your response was slow in coming, is difficult to express or explain, and leaves you confused, you are in a workplace where the direction is obscure and the future harbors doubt.

In that case The Planning Wheel model provides the tools you will need to close the gap between where you are and where you want to be.]

Figure 20 — Planning Wheel

The Planning Wheel

The Planning Wheel is a contemporary tool resembling a ship's helm, which controls the rudder, and therefore, the direction of the vessel. At the center of the wheel is the hub, representing the purpose of the voyage.

Radiating outward from the hub are the spokes of the wheel. These spokes represent bidirectional communication channels, connecting the hub with the rim of the wheel. At the intersection of each spoke and the rim lies a point of action. Each point represents an opportunity for Doers to exchange information, measure their progress, and report their observations.

The points of The Planning Wheel will be described in the context of how EPU applied each step to build and maintain its reputation for excellence.

1. DEFINE PURPOSE: Provide a clear, mental image of a preferred future state.

The purpose behind the EPU vision is that children grow up in families in which their individual needs are met; their parents have confidence in themselves and their ability to meet the needs of all family members and have a sense of comfort with their personal situations that brings forth an internal sense of empowerment.

From inception, the founder emphasized the importance of collaborative interaction between EPU, parents and all agencies providing services to the children with special needs. As the organization grew and more Doers were added it became apparent that in order to maintain the level of cooperation desired by the founder, a set of guiding principles were needed. The Tenets of Teamwork were introduced and developed in accordance with the following personal beliefs and operational practices:

Collaborative Spirit – Doers achieve more together than by working alone. Collaboration develops as goals and objectives are accomplished.

Mutual Respect – Mutual expectations are shared before action is taken. Doers focus on clarification and correction rather than on faultfinding.

Common Purpose – Doers work toward the same things at the same time. Problem solving and decision-making are applied simultaneously.

Productive Communication – Leaders clarify personal responsibilities and review authority, roles, and reporting relationships prior to taking action.

Neutral Attitude – Disagreements are resolved quickly. Recurring conflicts are set aside for future intervention and not allowed to block teamwork.

[Author note: Building an effective and fully functional team is the most critical part of a successful planning strategy. A clearly defined purpose statement defines why the team exists, what it has to offer, who it wishes to serve, and what it hopes to achieve. Without a published declaration of intention, much effort and energy will be wasted while leaders, coworkers or followers do their own thing their own way. The team building process should provide Doers with a charted vision and a sense of direction, while at the same time enabling them to remain flexible and responsive to the challenges of change.]

2. DEFINE GOALS & OBJECTIVES: Determine the appropriate number of tasks to be accomplished.

Rather than continuously strive to set higher goals and overcome funding challenges in response to the competitive performance demands, EPU leaders and followers instead developed an equation that enabled Doers to communicate truthfully, to make future-focused decisions, and to solve problems collaboratively.

The leader-follower equation empowered the EPU leadership team to think strategically about the highest and best use of the funds that were placed in their care.

Emboldened by the leader-follower equation, the leadership team, under the founder's guidance, became proficient in knowing how to track and compare which objectives were being met and which were not. Their collective ability to review performance expectations and prepare corrective action plans sent a clear message to current and potential funding sources that EPU's future would continue to be thoughtfully crafted and professionally orchestrated regardless of who occupied the director's chair.

The long term benefits of this outcome-focused strategy lessened the negative side effects resulting from goal ambiguity; contributed to the formation of a Doer-friendly culture where sustainable improvement occurred naturally; helped both sides of the leader-follower equation to understand the difference between a worthy objective and a fruitless aspiration; and most importantly provided the founder and her leadership team with the insight into how to sustain a vibrant, dynamic, and energized workforce.

[Author note: Goals and objectives define the amount of work or number of tasks a work unit or individual is expected to complete, the resources to be expended, the degree of accuracy needed, and the manner in which the team or individuals should

conduct themselves as they perform their duties. Goals state what the targets are and how often each needs to be accomplished. Objectives provide a sense of direction that helps both sides of the leader-follower equation to stay aligned with the organization's purpose.]

3. DEFINE PRIORITIES: Determine the order in which each task is to be completed.

Like any well-run organization, EPU was constantly faced with the challenge of handling multiple objectives and competing priorities. Included in the succession planning strategy was an intensive coaching and Doer-led mentoring program designed to raise the level of expertise and the understanding of change management throughout the organization.

The purpose of this educational effort was to help participants develop the skills and abilities to maintain organizational growth and achieve maximum individual and departmental potential.

The founder's leadership team responded quickly to this organization-wide learning opportunity by pinpointing roles, relationships, and reporting responsibilities associated with specific program functions and work tasks.

Additionally, EPU staff and professional service providers came away from this enhanced learning experience with new skills that enabled them to:

- Confidently size up problems and select priority-based solutions.
- Successfully execute change leadership principles, tools, and techniques.

- Implement processes for planning and improving performance.
- Apply motivational and behavioral techniques that transform others.

[Author note: Prioritizing work assignments and supporting tasks establishes the importance of each goal and objective. It determines the order in which specific actions are to be undertaken. When resources are limited and deadlines are pressing, a set of well-defined priorities enables Doers to decide which goals are immediate and which can be set aside temporarily. Attaching priorities empowers Doers to calculate the cost-benefit of alternate actions. Thus informed, both sides of the leader-follower equation can react to change quickly and smoothly by shifting priorities or setting new goals and objectives.]

4. ESTABLISH MINIMUM ACCEPTABLE RESULTS: Document baseline performance standards.

As the demand from a growing list of funding sources for more detailed reporting increased EPU managers were provided with a set of easy-to-use feedback tools that helped to expose whatever might be blocking an individual's performance or a work unit's productivity.

Once these factors are opened up for discussion, both the leader and the impacted followers were better able to understand how best to unblock the performance pathway to improved outcomes.

The least threatening way to introduce Performance Management and Process Improvement throughout EPU's operational structure was to frame a sequence of questions in the form of a checklist that followed the natural workflow:

a) Is the right person in the right job doing the right thing the right way for the right reason?

b) Is the right thing getting to the right place at the right time in the right quantity and the right condition?

An integral part of the Doer-led coaching process for underachievers included an awareness of why getting it right was important coupled with an understanding of what changes they need to make in order to have a future with EPU. Under-performers and their peer coaches would then co-jointly work their way through the checklists until they could both confidently answer yes.

It was a common practice for underachievers to come away from a performance coaching session with a better understanding of what was expected of them and a readiness to consider the highest and best use of their skills and abilities.

As programs expanded and new people were hired, the program managers briefed their new employees on how individual performance related to collective productivity.

[Author note: Under pressure, routine tasks are often overlooked in favor of higher priorities. Failure to maintain balance and achieve minimum standards is the primary source of bottlenecks, production stoppages, and work slowdowns. Without a set of minimum standards Doers are likely to let some vital tasks go while they focus on their own priorities. Knowing how to balance one's

efforts between minimum results and high priorities is vital to ones ability to achieve organizational goals and objectives.]

5. ASSIGN MANAGEMENT ACCOUNTABILITY: Pinpoint authority, roles, and reporting relationships.

Holding Doers accountable during a change in executive leadership demanded that EPU program managers not only keep abreast of current circumstances and the environment around them, but also that they acquire a mental model or mind set that enabled them to make decisions and take corrective action without hesitation.

With this objective in mind EPU program managers were trained in the use of Responsibility Charting and Task Mapping to assist them in the recognition and resolution of accountability issues.

Responsibility Charting is a powerful diagnostic tool that keeps track of specific functions and work task roles, reporting relationships, and responsibilities. As new programs were funded and established programs expanded EPU managers found this to be powerful tool because it enabled them to launch new services in a timely manner without diverting resources from existing programs.

Task Mapping provided Doers with the structure for collaboration. It could be applied either verbally in an informative manner or formally with matrix charts and documents. Program managers realized that gathering Doers together and walking them through the task mapping process quickly cleared up misunderstandings.

In an effort to support those who were often fully engaged in their day-to-day obligations process consultants were occasionally brought in to identify systems issues that may be hampering improvement efforts.

These outside specialists collaborated with the leadership team to determine which of the following methodologies should be applied to restore productive interactions within the program that needed attention:

Force Field Analysis: look at existing system dynamics and program productivity from all perspectives to find ways to blend and capitalize on existing resources.

Conflict Management: recognize that both interpersonal and interdepartmental conflicts exist; identify the cause of these disagreements, and develop mutually agreeable solutions.

Trust Building: resolve internal and external problems that may be negatively impacting individual responsiveness and thereby develop more collaborative working relationships.

[Author note: Without a structured planning process that originates at the upper levels an organization lacks the means of tracking accountability for unmet expectations. One way to expedite management accountability under such conditions is to assign it yourself. Start by submitting your carefully crafted plan to your supervisor with the stipulation that unless you are directed otherwise you intend to move forward. The longer he or she ponders the issue of authorship, the more time you have to prove the worthiness of your ideas. Once those above you see the positive results, they are bound to step forward and approve the plan. After that, you are in a position to accept

it if you know what will work, or delegate it upward
if you need more time to test your ideas.]

6. DEFINE PERFORMANCE METRICS: Develop key result areas to guide performance.

Key Result Areas (KRAs) refer to the outcomes or outputs for which someone is held responsible. Identifying KRAs within each program area helps Doers to clarify their respective roles and to ensure that their goals are aligned with the founder's vision.

KRAs typically capture about 80% of a work role. The remainder of the role is usually devoted to areas of shared responsibility such as helping team members, attending meetings, and participating in fund raising activities.

To guide EPU program managers, supervisors, and staff in the development and implementation of the KRA process, the mission of each program was broken down into measurable components by responsibility.

Performance Indicators were determined and a standard or target was set. A timetable for completion was agreed upon and coordination requirements were formalized and submitted to the program manager for approval.

Implementing KRA's enabled the executive leadership team to focus on results rather than activities and behaviors. Armed with a list of KRAs applicable to their specific area of responsibility, Doers were better able to communicate the purpose and intention of their roles and their relationship to other programs.

Once the KRA process was fully operational, Doers found it easier to set goals and objectives, make value-added decisions, and prioritize activities, which greatly enhanced their management of time and allocation of resources.

[Author note: A key result area provides measurable indicators for how much time and effort it should take to achieve each performance goal. Knowing what to focus on is the key to meeting expectations. Doers need to know how much energy to expend in order to reach the goal. Also, they will want to know which indicators will be used to measure their performance. Hard indicators, such as budget, quotas, errors, profits, sales, expenses, and deadlines, can be applied to measure efficiency. Soft indicators, such as satisfaction, experience, confidence, attitude, values, spirit, and motivation, typically measure effectiveness.]

7. ESTABLISH PERFORMANCE FEEDBACK: Provide an objective review of accomplishments.

During a period of transition like the one EPU was going through in preparation for the founder's retirement, organizational communication, both formal and informal, must focus on clarification, disclosure, and feedback.

To ensure the accuracy and reliability of information moving up and down the chain of command a Communication Monitoring Team (CMT) consisting of peer-supported, management-appointed Doers from all programs was formed to identify any misconceptions or misunderstandings that may be hampering organizational effectiveness.

The CMT met monthly to take the pulse of the organization as it moved through the succession planning process. The CMT had no decision-making authority and was not intended to suggest a course of action. Its purpose was to facilitate internal communication and to do three other important things:

- Demonstrate that the leadership team wanted to know how things are going for their followers.
- Serve as a focus group to review plans and directives before they were announced to staff.
- Provide program managers with the opportunity to clarify misconceived or misapplied directives and to counter potentially harmful rumors.

When Doers trust the formal communication pathways to be reliable, they are more likely to believe that what they say matters, that they are important to EPU's future, that they have ideas worth listening to, and that they are and will continue to be a valued resource.

[*Author note: Keep track of which objectives are or are not being met. Observations from managers, coworkers, customers, suppliers and others in supportive roles provide an objective view. Fair and frequent feedback is best. Doers want to know how they are doing. They are particularly interested in finding out when they are not meeting their performance objectives. To have meaning feedback must be fair, objective, and timely. One way to ensure fairness is to involve more observers. If the feedback contains observations from coworkers, customers, suppliers, and employees in other departments, in addition to the supervisor, it would provide a well-rounded and objective view.*]

8. AUDIT GOALS & OBJECTIVES: Identify what worked, what failed, and why.

As EPU's reputation for quality care spread, more and more families with children who had special needs sought support and assistance. Being the best attracts attention, which was a good thing, but it also presented a dilemma for EPU leaders as they struggled to determine how best to allocate their limited resources so as not to turn away any family or deprive any children of the care they needed.

Responding to the increased demands not only required additional resources, but also meant that EPU would have to expand its funding base to include larger agencies and private foundations that offered multiyear grants.

Receiving larger sums from these bigger agencies also came with stricter guidelines; more detailed reporting and record keeping, and higher performance expectations. The EPU leadership responded to this challenge by taking the steps necessary to ensure that their respective programs were thoughtfully planned and skillfully directed.

Strategic thinking was introduced as a systematic process for making long-range decisions. The leadership team underwent coaching and consultation to hone these necessary skills and to further develop their ability to:

- Make future-focused decisions with a higher degree of certainty.

- Organize systematically to carry out these decisions.

- Measure the results of these decisions against initial expectations.

- Create an environment where leaders and followers think and act strategically—in every decision and every action, every day.

[Author note: A review of individual and collective performance expectations should point out which goals and objectives were difficult to achieve and which were relatively easy. This offers a great opportunity to uncover any dysfunctional side effects resulting from goal ambiguity, resource conflicts, or role confusion. Some Doers may be suffering or stressed from overload, while the less productive employees may need greater challenges to keep them motivated and engaged. Provide recognition to those who met or exceeded their targets. Prepare corrective action plans including training and development, or remedial discipline for those with results lower that expected.]

9. UNATTAINABLE GOALS & OBJECTIVES: Determine the potential of further investment.

The pervasive challenge for the founder's leadership team throughout EPU's history has been how to overcome future challenges without losing sight of past successes.

It was time now for them to take stock of what had been accomplished over the past three-plus decades and to think strategically about how best to ensure that the founder's legacy would continue long past her pending retirement.

An analysis of Strengths, Weaknesses, Opportunities, and Threats (SWOT) was selected as the best way to examine and integrate internal and external environments.

Strengths: those aspects of the organization that serve EPU well. These include what it does well, what it is known for, what it takes pride in as well as those competencies or characteristics that need to be enhanced or preserved.

Weaknesses: areas that, if not addressed, could become liabilities or could contribute to an erosion of EPU's capacities and potential growth. They represent areas where the organization needs to improve if it is to be successful for the long term.

Opportunities: trends and events occurring outside EPU that if taken advantage of are likely to have a positive effect on its long-term success. Although opportunities may be gifts from the external environment, the organization must be assertive or even aggressive in pursuing and taking advantage of them.

Threats: trends and events occurring outside EPU that could jeopardize its success. Identifying threats provides an opportunity to highlight EPU's relationship with customers, emphasize its quality or reintroduce the organization to the community.

The SWOT analysis revealed emerging issues and trends that were affecting the current status and future growth potential of EPU. Armed with this knowledge the leadership team developed responses and strategies that proactively prepared for these issues.

The information gleaned from the environmental scan was not only vital to the current administration, but would also be of great value to whoever was selected to replace the founder when she turned over the helm.

[Author note: Examine closely what is not working and determine why. Then decide what can be done to change the outcome and how much time, talent, and treasure will be needed to ensure success. Assemble the Doers and discuss which goals and objectives is a waste of their efforts and which could be salvaged. Decide whether these goals are worth any further investment and determine where those resources are to be found. Should attainment of a goal still be important, identify the constraints that are blocking success and find ways to remove these barriers or lessen the impact they are having on performance outcomes.]

Confirming The Purpose

The action points around the rim of The Planning Wheel provided the EPU leadership team with the opportunity to exchange and review vital information and feedback from staff, volunteers, vendors, and funders. This interactive system is what gives The Planning Wheel its flexibility. It allows the purpose to be continuously reassessed in response to internal and external demands for improvement.

EPU employees at all levels were trained to enter The Planning Wheel from any point on the rim. For instance, when a new program manager joined the leadership team, he or she would typically plug in at Stage 8 by looking at the current goals and objectives. Once the assessment was complete, the new manager could either support the continuation of the work in progress or make changes to the processes currently in place.

Whenever a new program was launched and there were no stated goals and objectives, new managers were encouraged to enter at Stage 1 or 2. In either situation, it is important for them to make a good first impression. Taking the advice of veteran Doers, new managers learned quickly that gathering their followers around The Planning Wheel was a great way to establish their authority and to improve the outcomes within their sphere of influence.

During periods of growth and progression over the span of three decades EPU held fast to the founder's vision and regularly brought in program consultants and treatment specialists to update its mission, goals, and objectives.

Without the constant reinforcement of the founder's original purpose, it would have been easy for those joining the organization over the years to lose their way or become distracted by the growing complexity and the challenges of change. Such was not the case at EPU, however, because the founder understood the importance of creating a workplace where Doers would flourish and the organization would prosper as a result.

There is no doubt Marian Karian will be missed, but thanks to her inspirational leadership and the dedication of her devoted followers and loyal supporters, her legacy will live long in the hearts and minds of the many children and families whose lives she touched.

About the Author

Dr. Tom E. Jones has spent three decades consulting with Fortune 500 companies and small businesses alike striving to create workplaces where Doers are highly prized.

As a leadership coach and career mentor Jones shows management how to guide, encourage, and support Doers so that their natural desire to succeed is fully utilized. Doers themselves learn how to identify workplaces where their enthusiasm for excellence is recognized and rewarded.

Tom has studied organizations and the people they employ long enough to have a keen sense of what it takes for both to prosper. He writes and speaks about those operational struggles that ultimately determine the success or failure of a modern organization.

Jones uses real life stories to convey his insight into the mind-numbing uncertainty that exists in today's workplace. So accurate are his observations, so helpful are his solutions; audiences wonder whether he has been quietly watching their workplace.

His writings have appeared in The Wall Street Journal, American City Business Journals, Executive Excellence, Fortune, and Entrepreneur, Smart Money and Inc. magazines. Tom authors The Doers Blog which is available on his website www.worxinc.com.

Thanks to his award winning books, *If It's Broken, You Can Fix It — Help! I'm Surrounded By Idiots — Doer's Dilemma* and his recent release *DOERS: New Game-Changers*, Tom's insightful message is reaching an ever-expanding audience.

Jones holds a Doctoral degree in Organization and Leadership from the University of San Francisco. He has taught at six universities and currently lectures on the Principles of Management for the College of Business at California State University, Monterey Bay.